CHINESE FOLKTALES

In the same series

BRETON FOLKTALES

RUSSIAN FOLKTALES

PERSIAN FOLKTALES

Chinese Folktales

LONDON: G. BELL & SONS 1971

PRINTED IN GREAT BRITAIN BY
NORTHUMBERLAND PRESS LTD, GATESHEAD

ISBN 0 7135 1813 8

ORIGINALLY PUBLISHED AS CHINESISCHE MÄRCHEN TRANS-
LATED INTO GERMAN BY RICHARD WILHELM, 1958 THIS
SELECTION TRANSLATED FROM THE GERMAN BY
EWALD OSERS

CONTENTS

1. Flesh and blood divided by a woman's words   9
2. The child of good fortune and the child of ill fortune   12
3. The nine-headed bird   14
4. The animals' cave   18
5. The fox and the tiger   21
6. The tiger's bait   22
7. The fox and the raven   23
8. Why the dog and the cat are enemies   24
9. Yang Erlh-Lang   26
10. No Chia   29
11. The Queen of Heaven   38
12. Nü Wa   41
13. Confucius   45
14. The God of War   50
15. Haloes   54
16. Lao-tse   56
17. The priest of Lau Shan   58
18. The mean peasant   63
19. A punishment for disbelief   65
20. Morning Sky   67
21. King Mu of Chou   72
22. Old Chiang   76
23. The kindly magician   81
24. How Mu Lien got his mother out of Hell   88
25. The flower spirits   90

26. The spirit of the Wulien mountain   95
27. The spirit of the Horse mountain   96
28. The little dog   99
29. The dragon emerging from hibernation   102
30. The spirits of Yellow River   103
31. Help in need   112
32. The rejected princess   121
33. The fox hole   131
34. Fox fire   134
35. The fox and the thunder   136
36. The kind fox and the wicked fox   138
37. Great Father Hu   142
38. The talking silver foxes   144
39. The necromancer   147
40. Ghost stories   150
41. The land of the ogres   153
42. The girl who was abducted   161
43. The flying ogre   164
44. Black magic   166
45. The faithful girl   173
46. The painted skin   178
47. The sect of the White Lotus   185
48. How three heroes died for the sake of two
    peaches   188
49. Old Dragon-beard   191
50. How Molo stole Rose-red   199

Notes   205

1. FLESH AND BLOOD DIVIDED BY A
WOMAN'S WORDS

ONCE there were two brothers who shared the same house. The tall one always listened to his wife and this led to a quarrel with his brother. Summer had come and it was time to sow the tall millet. But the short one had no grain and he therefore asked the tall one if he would lend him some. The tall one commanded his wife to do so. But the wife took the grain, put it in a large pot and boiled it. Then she gave it to the short one. The short one unknowingly went out and sowed the grain on his field. But as the grain had been boiled no shoots sprouted forth. Only one single seed had escaped being cooked entirely; and so a single shoot sprouted up. The short one was hard-working and conscientious by nature and he therefore watered and hoed the shoot all day long. And so it grew up into a mighty tree and it bore a spike as large as a canopy, shading half an acre of land. In the autumn it ripened. Then the short one took an axe and chopped down the spike. But no sooner had the spike dropped to the ground than a gigantic roc arrived with a rushing of wings, picked it up in its beak and flew off. The short one ran after it all the way to the edge of the sea.

The bird turned round and addressed him in a human voice: 'Do not harm me. Surely one spike is not worth much to you. East of the sea lies the island of gold and silver. I will carry you there. There you can take as much as you like and become exceedingly rich.'

The short one agreed and climbed on the bird's back.

9

The bird told him to close his eyes. All he could hear was the rushing of the air past his ears, as though he was travelling through a mighty wind, and below him he could hear the roaring and raging of billowing waves. Presently the bird landed on an island. 'We have arrived,' it said.

Then the short one opened his eyes and looked around him. Everything gleamed and glittered, all was yellow and white. He picked up about a dozen of the smaller lumps and placed them inside his shirt.

'Is that enough?' the roc asked.

'Yes, I have enough,' he replied.

"Well done,' said the bird. 'Moderation will guard you against harm.'

Then the bird took him on its back again and carried him home over the sea.

After his return the short one bought himself a good patch of land and became fairly prosperous.

His brother, however, grew envious and taunted him: 'Where did you steal that money?'

The short one told him the whole truth. Then the tall one went home and consulted with his wife.

'Nothing easier,' said the wife. 'I will simply boil the grain again and keep one grain back so it does not get cooked. You will then sow that grain and we shall see what will happen.'

No sooner said than done: sure enough, a single shoot grew up and that shoot bore a single spike, and when harvest time came the roc again appeared and carried it off in its beak. The tall one was delighted and ran after it and the roc again spoke the same words as before and carried the tall one to the island. There he saw mountains of gold and silver all round him. The largest lumps were like mountains, the smaller ones were like bricks and the very small ones like grains of sand. His eyes were blinded by the glitter. He wished that he knew how to move mountains. So he bent down and picked up whatever lumps he could.

The roc said: 'That is enough now! The load is getting too heavy for you.'

'Be patient a little longer,' said the tall one. 'Don't be in such a hurry! I must have a few more pieces.'

And so the time passed.

The roc again urged him to hurry. 'The sun will be up presently,' it said, 'and then all human beings are scorched by its fierce heat.'

'Give me just a little longer,' said the tall one.

But at that instant a red wheel arose mightily. The roc flew into the sea, spread out both its wings and beat the water with them so as to escape the heat. But the tall one was consumed by the sun.

ONCE upon a time there was a proud ruler who had a daughter. But the daughter was a child of ill fortune. When the time came for her to marry she ordered all her suitors to assemble before her father's castle. She was to throw a red silken ball among them and whoever caught it would become her husband. Many princes and counts assembled before the castle. Yet among them there was also a beggar. And the princess saw that small dragons were crawling into his ears and emerging through his nose; for he was a child of good fortune. So she threw the ball to the beggar and he caught it.

Angrily her father demanded: 'Why did you throw the ball into the beggar's hands?'

'He is a child of good fortune,' said the princess. 'I want to marry him, and then perhaps I shall share in his good fortune.'

But the father would not hear of it, and when she stood firm he drove her from the castle in anger.

So the princess had to go off with the beggar. She lived with him in his small hut and had to gather herbs and roots and cook them herself so they should have something to eat. Often they both went hungry.

One day her husband said to her: 'I shall go out and seek my fortune. When I have found it I will return for you.' The princess said: 'Yes,' and he left. He was away for eighteen years. And the princess lived in want and sorrow, for her father remained hard and unyielding. If her mother had not secretly sent her money and food she might well have died of hunger during that long period.

The beggar, however, made his fortune and eventually became emperor. He returned and stood before his wife. But she no longer recognized him. She only knew that he was the emperor.

He asked her how she was.

'Why do you ask me how I am?' she replied. 'Surely I am much too lowly for you.'

'Who then is your husband?'

'My husband was a beggar. He left to seek his fortune. Eighteen years have passed now and he has still not returned.'

'And what have you been doing all this long time?'

'I have been waiting for his return.'

'Have you no wish to take another husband since he has stayed away so long?'

'No, I shall remain his wife unto death.'

When the emperor saw how faithful his wife was he revealed himself to her, had her arrayed in fine garments and took her with him to his imperial castle. There they then lived in splendour and joy.

After a few days the emperor said to his wife: 'We spend each day feasting, just as though it were the New Year.'

'And why should we not spend our time feasting,' the woman replied, 'now that we are emperor and empress?'

But the woman was a child of ill fortune after all. When she had been empress for eighteen days she fell ill and died. But the man lived for many more years.

A LONG time ago there lived a king and queen who had a daughter. One day the daughter was walking in the garden, when suddenly a tremendous storm arose and carried her away. But the storm had come from the nine-headed bird. The bird carried off the princess and took her to its cave. The king did not know where his daughter had vanished to. So he ordered a proclamation to be read throughout the land: 'Whoever brings me back my daughter, shall have her for his wife.'

A young man had seen the bird carrying the king's daughter to its cave. But the cave was halfway up a steep rock face. No one could climb up to it from the bottom or descend to it from the top. As the young man was pacing around the rock another man came along and asked him what he was doing. He told him that the nine-headed bird had carried off the king's daughter and taken her to the cave in the mountain. The other man knew what to do. He called his friends and together they let the young man down to the cave in a basket. As he entered the cave he saw the king's daughter sitting there, bathing the wound of the nine-headed bird. The hound of heaven had bitten off its tenth head and the wound was still bleeding. The princess, however, motioned the young man to hide. This he did. The bird felt so much at ease while the king's daughter was bathing its wound and bandaging it that all its nine heads fell asleep one after the other. Then the man stepped out from his hiding-place and with one sword cut off all the bird's heads. He led the princess

14

outside and wanted her to be raised in the basket. But the king's daughter said: 'It would be better if you went up first and I followed you.'

'No,' said the young man. 'I will wait down here until you are safe.'

At first the princess was reluctant, but then she allowed herself to be persuaded and stepped into the basket. Before doing so, however, she took a long hairpin and broke it in two, giving one half to the young man and keeping the other herself. She also divided her silken kerchief with him and bade him guard both things carefully. But when the other man had hauled the king's daughter up to the top he took her with him and left the young man in the cave in spite of all his shouting and pleading.

The young man now inspected the cave. He saw a great many maidens who had been carried off by the nine-headed bird and had died there of hunger. On the wall was a fish, pinned to it with four nails. When he touched the fish it changed into a handsome young man who thanked him for rescuing him. The two young men pledged lifelong brotherhood to each other. Soon the young man felt the pangs of hunger. He stepped outside the cave to look for food but all he could see was stones. Suddenly he caught sight of a great dragon licking a stone. The young man likewise licked the stone and soon his hunger was gone. He then asked the dragon how he could escape from the cave. The dragon nodded his head towards his tail and motioned him to sit down on it. The young man stepped on the dragon's tail and in a trice he was down on the ground and the dragon had disappeared. He continued on his way and found a tortoise-shell full of beautiful pearls. But these pearls had magic powers: if they were thrown on a fire the fire stopped burning, if they were cast on the water the water parted so one could walk through it. The young man took the pearls from the tortoise-shell and put them in his pocket. A short while afterwards he came to the edge of the sea. He flung in one pearl; the sea divided and he caught sight of the sea dragon. The dragon exclaimed: 'Who is that disturbing me here in my realm?' The young man replied: 'I found some pearls in a tortoise-shell and cast them on the sea and the water parted before me.'

'If that is so,' said the dragon, 'then come down into the sea to me and we shall live together.' Then the young man realized that this was the same dragon which he had seen in the cave. The young man to whom he had pledged brotherhood was also there. He was the dragon's son.

'You saved my son and pledged yourself to be his brother; so I shall be your father,' said the old dragon. And he treated him to wine and food.

One day his friend said to him: 'No doubt my father will wish to reward you. But accept no money, nor precious stones. Simply take that small pumpkin flask over there—with that you can conjure up whatever you wish.'

Sure enough, the old dragon asked him what he would like as a reward and the young man replied: 'Neither money nor precious stones, simply that small gourd flask.'

At first the dragon did not want to give it to him. But in the end he did, and the young man left the dragon's castle.

When he reached dry land again he felt hungry. Presently a table stood before him, laden with delicious food. The young man ate and drank. He had gone on for a while when he felt tired. At once a donkey stood before him and he climbed on its back. When he had ridden for a little while the donkey became too bumpy for him; at once a carriage appeared and he stepped inside. But the carriage too jolted too much for him and he thought: 'If only I had a sedan chair! That would be better!' And at once there was a sedan chair and the young man got inside. The bearers took him all the way to the city where the king, the queen and their daughter lived.

When the other man returned the princess to the king preparations were made for their wedding. But the king's daughter had no wish to marry him and said: 'This is not yet the right man. My rescuer will come, he has half my hairpin and half my kerchief as tokens.' But when after a long time the young man failed to appear, the other pressed the king, who grew impatient and said: 'The wedding shall be tomorrow!' Sadly the king's daughter walked through the streets of the city, searching for the man who had saved her. On that very day the sedan chair arrived. The king's daughter saw half the kerchief in the young man's hand. Full of joy she took him to her father. He had to produce his half of the hairpin and this matched exactly the other half. Then the king believed that this was the right man. The false bridegroom was punished, the wedding was celebrated, and they lived joyously and happily ever after.

ONCE there was a couple who had seven daughters. One day the father went out to collect firewood and found seven wild duck eggs. He took them home with him but he did not intend to give them to his children. He wanted to eat them all with his wife. Towards evening the eldest daughter woke up and asked her mother what she was cooking. Her mother said: 'I am cooking wild duck eggs. I'll give you one, but you must not tell your sisters.' And she gave her one. At that moment the second daughter awoke and asked her mother what she was cooking. She said: 'Wild duck eggs. If you won't tell your sisters, I'll give you one.' And so it continued. In the end the daughters had eaten up all the eggs and none were left.

In the morning the father was very angry with his children and said: 'Who is coming with me to your grandmother's?' But he really wanted to take the children into the mountains and leave them there to be devoured by the wolves. The eldest daughters suspected this and said: 'We are not coming.' But the two youngest said: 'We'll go with you.' They set out with their father. When they had driven in the donkey cart for a long time they asked: 'When are we getting to grandmother's?' Their father said: 'Soon.' And when they had got into the mountains the father said: 'You wait here. I am going ahead to the village to tell your grandmother you are coming.' And he drove off. The girls waited and waited, but their father did not return. In the end they realized that he was

18

not coming back for them and had left them in the mountains alone. They wandered on farther into the mountains, seeking shelter for the night. They chose a large stone for a pillow. They were about to roll it to the spot where they wanted to lie down and sleep when they saw that the stone was the door to a cave. From the cave came a glow of light and they went in. The light came from a mass of precious stones and jewels of all kinds. The cave belonged to a wolf and fox, who had many pots full of precious stones and pearls which glowed by night. So the girls said: 'This is a fine cave, let us lie down on the beds straight away.' For there were two golden beds there, with gold-embroidered covers. And they lay down on them and fell asleep. During the night the wolf and the fox returned. The wolf said: 'I can smell human flesh.' The fox said: 'Human flesh? Never! No humans can get into our cave. It's much too well hidden.' And the wolf said: 'Well then, let's go to bed and sleep.' But the fox said: 'Let's lie down in the cauldrons on the fire. There is still some warmth in them.' One of the cauldrons was of gold and the other of silver. So they lay down in them.

When the girls got up in the morning they saw the fox and the wolf lying there and were much afraid. So they covered the cauldrons and piled a great many big stones on the lids so the wolf and the fox could not get out again. Then they lit the fire. The wolf and the fox said: 'What a nice warm morning! How can that be?' But soon they were too hot. They discovered that the two girls had lit the fire and they called out: 'Let us out! We'll give you plenty of precious stones and a pile of gold and we shan't do you any harm.' But the girls did not listen to them and built up the fire even higher, So the wolf and the fox died in the cauldrons.

For many days the girls lived happily in the cave. But the father was seized with a longing to see his daughters again and went out into the mountains to look for them. He had just sat down on the stone outside the cave to rest himself and was knocking the ash from his pipe. Then the girls called out from inside: 'Who is that knocking at our door?' And the father said: 'Aren't those my daughters' voices?' And the daughters called: 'Isn't that our father's voice?' So they moved away the stone and saw that it was their father, and their father was happy to see them again. He was astonished to see them in this cave full of pearls and precious stones, and they told him everything. So the father went and got neighbours to help him carry the precious stones home, and when they returned the wife was amazed to see all these treasures. Then the father and his daughters told her the whole story and they became a very rich family and lived happily for the rest of their days.

5. THE FOX AND THE TIGER

ONE day a fox encountered a tiger. The tiger showed his fangs and waved his claws and wanted to eat him up. But the fox said: 'Good sir, you must not think that you alone are the king of beasts. Your courage is no match for mine. Let us go on together and you keep behind me. If the humans are not afraid of me when they see me, then you may eat me up.'

The tiger agreed and so the fox led him to a big highway. As soon as the travellers saw the tiger in the distance they were seized with fear and ran away.

Then the fox said: 'You see? I was walking in front, they saw me before they could see you.'

Then the tiger put his tail between his legs and ran away.

The tiger had seen that the humans were afraid of the fox but he had not realized that the fox had merely borrowed his own terrible appearance.

6. THE TIGER'S BAIT

THE fox borrowing the tiger's terrible appearance is only a parable, but the tiger's bait is something one reads about frequently in history books and hears grandfathers talk about—so there must be some truth in it. It is said that whenever a tiger eats a human his spirit cannot escape and the tiger uses it as a bait. When he goes out marauding the spirit of his victim must walk in front to hide him, so that the people don't see the tiger. The spirit may then turn into a beautiful girl or a lump of gold or silken raiments. All kinds of illusions are used to decoy humans into the mountain gorges. Then the tiger appears and devours his victim. The spirit of his new victim must then become his bait and the old one is released from his services and is allowed to depart. In this way the chain continues.

People who are forced by cunning and powerful men to allow themselves to be used to the detriment of others are therefore called 'the tiger's bait'.

7. THE FOX AND THE RAVEN

THE fox is a past master of flattery and cunning. One day he saw a raven settling on a tree, with a piece of meat in its beak. The fox sat down under the tree, looked up to the raven and began to praise him.

'Your colour,' he began, 'is pure black; that shows that you have the wisdom of Lao-tse who knows how to preserve his obscurity. The manner in which you feed your mother proves that your filial piety equals Master Chung's solicitude for his parents. Your voice is harsh and strong; that shows that you possess the courage of king Hsiang who turned his enemies to flight by the mere sound of his voice. You are indeed the king of birds.'

The raven was delighted to hear this and said : 'You're too kind!'

And before he knew it he had dropped the piece of meat from his opened beak.

The fox caught it, ate it up, laughed and said : 'Remember this, my friend : Whenever anyone sings your praises without cause you may be sure he is after something.'

A MAN and his wife had a golden ring. It was a lucky ring and whoever owned it always had enough to live on, but they did not know this and sold the ring for a small sum of money. No sooner was the ring out of the house than they started to become poorer and poorer, and in the end they did not know where their next meal was coming from. They also had a dog and a cat, and these had to go hungry with them. The animals thereupon took counsel with each other about how they could help the humans to recapture their former good luck. In the end the dog came up with an idea.

'They must get the ring back,' he said to the cat.

The cat said: 'The ring is kept in a casket where no one can get at it.'

'You catch a mouse,' said the dog. 'The mouse must gnaw through the casket and get the ring out. Tell it that unless it does your bidding you will bite it dead, and then it will obey.'

The cat liked this advice and went to catch a mouse. With the mouse in its teeth the cat set out for the house where the casket was kept and the dog followed behind. They soon came to a great river. And because the cat could not swim the dog took it on his back and swam across with it. The cat carried the mouse to the house in which the casket was. The mouse gnawed a hole through the side of the casket and got the ring out. The cat took the ring in its mouth and returned to the river where the dog was waiting for it and once more swam across with it. Then they walked back home together to take the lucky ring to their master and mistress.

But the dog could only run along the ground; whenever a house stood in his way he had to run round it. The cat, on the other hand, ran swiftly up the walls and over the roofs and so got home long before the dog and took the ring to its master.

Then the master said to his wife: 'This cat is a good animal, we will always give it plenty of food and look after it as if it were our own child.'

When the dog got back home they beat him and up-braided him for not having helped to recover the ring. And the cat sat by the stove, preening itself and saying nothing. So the dog grew angry with the cat for having cheated him out of his reward and whenever he saw it he would chase it and try to pounce on it.

Since that day the dog and the cat have been enemies.

ONCE upon a time the second daughter of the lord of heaven descended to earth and there lived secretly with a mortal human named Yang. When she returned to heaven she gave birth to a son. The lord of heaven was very angry at this desecration of heaven. He banished her to earth and covered her with the Wu Yi mountain. But their son, by name of Erlh-lang, the grandson of the lord of heaven, was exceedingly gifted by nature. By the time he grew to manhood he had learnt the secret art of performing eight times nine transformations. He could make himself invisible or assume whatever shape among birds and beasts, grasses and trees, snakes and fishes he chose. He also knew how to drain the sea and move mountains. Thus he came to the Wu Yi mountain and rescued his mother. He took her on his back and carried her off. They halted on a ledge of rock.

The mother said: 'I am very thirsty.'

Erlh-lang descended into the valley to fetch water and before long he was back again. But his mother was no longer where he had left her. He looked for her everywhere and then found her skin and bones lying on the rock and a few traces of blood. At that time, of course, there were still ten suns in the sky and they shone and burnt like fire. Although the daughter of heaven was of divine nature, because she had fallen and bore the stain of having given birth, she had lost her magic powers. Moreover, she had been so long in the darkness beneath the mountain that, suddenly facing the sunlight, she was consumed by the suns' blinding glare.

As Erlh-lang reflected upon his mother's sad end his heart ached. He lifted two mountains upon his shoulders and pursued the suns and crushed them dead with the mountains. Whenever he had crushed a sun disc he would pick up a new mountain. Thus he had already killed nine of the ten suns. Only one was left. As Erlh-lang was pursuing it relentlessly it hid in despair under the leaves of the purslane. Erlh-lang searched for it in vain. But there was an earthworm nearby which betrayed the sun's hiding place by saying: 'There it is! There it is!'

Erlh-lang was about to seize it when suddenly a messenger descended from heaven with a command from the lord of heaven: 'Heaven, air and earth need sunshine. You must leave one sun in the sky so that all creatures may live. But since you rescued your mother and proved yourself a good son you shall be made a god and be my bodyguard in the highest hall of heaven, watching over good and evil in the world of humans, and with power over devils and demons.' When Erlh-lang had received this command he ascended to heaven.

Then the sun's disc reappeared from among the leaves of the purslane and out of gratitude to it granted it the gift of ready growth and immunity to sunshine. To this day one can see minute white pearls on its leaves: they are what is left of the sunshine which remained clinging to them from that time when the sun hid among its leaves. The earthworm, however, which had betrayed the sun, is pursued by it whenever it ventures out of the earth and dried out as a punishment.

Erlh-lang has been venerated as a god ever since. He has oblique sharp-cut eyebrows and in his hand is a three-pronged two-edged sword. By his side stand two servants with a falcon and a hound, for Erlh-lang is a great huntsman. The falcon is the falcon of the gods and the hound is the hound of heaven. Whenever animals achieve magic powers or when demons harass humans Erlh-lang tames them with his falcon and his hound.

THE eldest daughter of the lord of heaven had married the general Li Ching. Her sons were called Chin Chia, Mu Chia and No Chia. But before No Chia was born his mother had been carrying him for three years and six months. One night she dreamed that a Taoist priest entered her chamber. Angrily she bade him leave. But he said: 'Make haste to receive the divine son!' And with these words he placed a brilliant pear in her body. The woman had such a fright that she woke up. And there she gave birth to a ball of flesh which spun like a wheel, filling the chamber with strange perfumes and red light.

Li Ching was much startled and thought it was an evil spirit. With his sword he cleft the sphere in two and from it leapt a small boy whose whole body glowed with a rosy radiance. His face was delicate and as white as snow. On his right arm he wore a golden armlet, and tied round his hips was a piece of red silk so brilliant it blinded the eye. When Li Ching saw the child he took pity on him and did not kill him. And his wife conceived a deep love for the boy.

When three days had passed all their friends came to congratulate them. As they were all banqueting a Taoist priest entered and said: 'I am the Great One. This boy is the bright pearl of the first origin, lent to you as your son. But he is wild and uncontrolled and will kill many people. I will therefore take him as my pupil to pacify his wild nature.' Li Ching bowed gratefully and the Great One disappeared.

One day, when No Chia was seven years old he left home. He came to the nine-bend river whose green waters rolled along between two rows of weeping willows. It was a hot day and he stepped into the water to cool himself. He untied his red silk cloth and swished it through the water to wash it. All the water turned red from it. But as No Chia was sitting there, swishing his cloth in the water, the dragon king's castle in the eastern sea was shaken to its foundations. The dragon king therefore sent out a triton of horrible aspect to see what was happening. When it caught sight of the boy it began to scold him. But the boy glanced up and said: 'What a strange animal you are. Are you even capable of speech?' This infuriated the triton and it leapt up and hit out at No Chia with its axe. No Chia dodged the blow and flung his golden armlet at it. The armlet hit the triton on its head so that its brain spurted out and it fell down dead.

No Chia laughed: 'Now it has spattered my armlet with its blood.' And he sat down on a stone to wash it. Then the crystal castle of the dragon king began to shake until it was near to collapsing. A guard arrived and reported that the triton had been killed by a boy. So the dragon king sent out his son to question the boy. The son mounted the water-cleaving beast and arrived amidst a great roar of waves. No Chia straightened up and said: 'That's a good wave.' Suddenly he saw a beast emerging from the waves and on it a man in armour who shouted with a mighty voice: 'Who killed my triton?' No Chia replied: 'The triton tried to kill me, so I killed it. What is it to you?' Thereupon the dragon charged him with his halberd. But No Chia said: 'Tell me who you are before we start fighting.' 'I am the son of the dragon king,' was the reply. 'And I am No Chia, the son of the General Li

30

Ching. Now don't you make me angry with your violence or else I'll skin you alive, together with your old man, the mud fish!' This made the dragon furious and he charged savagely. But No Chia threw his red cloth into the air so that it flashed like a ball of fire and threw the young dragon from his mount. Then No Chia took his golden armlet and struck him on the forehead so that he had to reveal himself in his true shape of the golden dragon and he fell down dead.

No Chia laughed: 'I have heard it said that dragons' tendons make good rope. I will pull one out and bring it to my father so that he can fasten his armour with it.' And with these words he pulled out the dragon's dorsal tendon and took it home with him. Meanwhile the dragon king had hurried to No Chia's father Li Ching in wrath and demanded that he should hand his son over. But Li Ching said: 'You must be mistaken, my boy is only seven, he is incapable of such misdeeds.' While they were arguing No Chia came running up and called out: 'Father, here is a dragon's tendon I have brought you to fasten your armour with.' Thereupon the dragon king burst into tears and angry words of reproach. He threatened to denounce Li Ching to the lord of heaven and made off, snorting with anger.

Li Ching was greatly upset and told his wife about the incident; and both started to cry. But No Chia came in and said: 'What are you crying about? I will simply go to my master, the Great One, he will know what to do.' No sooner had he said these words than he was gone. He went up to his master and told him the whole story. The master said: 'You must get up to heaven before the dragon so he does not denounce you there.' Then he gave him some magic and No Chia was transported to the door of heaven, where he would wait for the dragon. It was still early in the morning. The door of heaven was not yet open and the guard had not yet arrived. And there the dragon came climbing up. No Chia, made invisible by his magic, threw the dragon to the ground by striking him from behind with his armlet and started to beat him. The dragon complained and screamed. 'Look how the old worm is squirming,' said No Chia, 'he does not seem to mind being beaten. I will scrape some of his scales off.' With these words he ripped open the dragon's ceremonial clothes and began to tear off some of his scales under his left arm so that the red blood began to drip. The dragon could not stand the pain any longer and asked for mercy. But No Chia did not let him go until he had promised not to denounce him. The dragon now had to change into a small green snake which No Chia slipped up his sleeve and so returned home. No sooner had he pulled the small snake out of his sleeve than it assumed human shape. The dragon swore frightful vengeance upon Li Ching and vanished in a flash of lightning.

Li Ching was seriously angry with his son. For that reason No Chia's mother sent him out of the way so his father should not see him. No Chia slipped away to his master to ask him what he should do if the dragon returned. He gave him his counsel and No Chia returned home. When he got back the dragon kings of all the four seas were assembled there and with much noise and shouting had tied up his parents to take their vengeance. No Chia raced up to them and shouted in a loud voice: 'Whatever I have done I shall answer for myself. No blame attaches to my parents. What satisfaction do you demand from me?'

'A life for a life!' shouted the dragon. 'Very well, I

will chop myself up. Will you promise me not to do my parents any harm then?' The dragon agreed and ordered the fetters of No Chia's parents to be struck. No Chia first hacked off one of his arms. His mother burst into loud lamentations. But it was of no avail. He had already slit open his body, his entrails spilled out, his three spirits and nine souls dispersed and his life returned to the beyond. Satisfied, the dragons departed and No Chia was buried by his mother with a great many tears.

But No Chia's spirit still fluttered about in the air and was carried by the wind to the cave of the Great One. He received him and said to him: 'You must appear to your mother. Forty miles from your home stands the green rock face. Upon that rock she is to build a temple to you. When you have enjoyed the incense of humans for three years you may receive a body again.' No Chia appeared to his mother in a dream and conveyed it all to her. She awoke wet with tears. But Li Ching was angry when she told him her dream. 'It serves that accursed boy right to be dead. But because you keep thinking of him he appears to you in your dream. You are not to take any notice of him.' The woman was silent, but from then onwards No Chia appeared to her every day the moment she closed her eyes and he became more and more insistent. In the end she had no other choice but to have a temple built for No Chia without Li Ching's knowledge.

In that temple No Chia performed great miracles. All prayers were answered. Men came from far and wide to burn incense to him.

Six months passed. Then one day Li Ching came by that mountain on a military exercise and saw the crowds swarming around the mountain like ants. Li Ching asked what there was to be seen there. 'There is a new god who works such miracles that people come from far and wide to revere him.' 'What kind of god is that?' asked Li Ching. They dared not keep the truth from him. Then Li Ching was angry. He galloped his horse up the mountain and there, true enough, over the temple gateway, was the inscription 'Temple of No Chia'. And inside was No Chia's picture, looking exactly as he had done while alive. Li Ching said: 'When you were alive you brought misfortune upon your parents. And now, after your death, you deceive the people. That is despicable!' With these words he drew his whip, shattered No Chia's idol, had the temple burnt down and pacified the worshippers. Then he returned home.

That day No Chia had been away in spirit. When he returned to his temple he found it in ruins. The spirit of the mountain told him what had happened. No Chia hurried to his master and, in tears, told him what had happened. The master said angrily: 'Li Ching was at fault. Once you have returned your body to your parents you are no longer any concern of theirs. Why should he deprive you of the enjoyment of incense?' Thereupon the Great One fashioned a body of lotus plants, breathed life into it and enclosed No Chia's spirit in this body. Then he called with a loud voice: 'Arise!' There came the sound of a breath and No Chia rose up again in the shape of a small boy. He threw himself down at his master's feet and thanked him. The master granted him the magic of the fiery lance and from then onwards No Chia had two whirling wheels under his feet—the wheel of wind and the wheel of fire. On these he could rise and descend in the air. The master also gave him a bag of panther skin to hold his armlet and red silk cloth.

Thoughts of revenge would not let No Chia rest. In

an unguarded moment he departed and on whirling wheels accompanied by the roar of thunder he made for Li Ching's home. Li Ching could not stand up to him and fled. His strength was about to leave him when out of the white crane's cave came his second son Mu Chia, the disciple of the holy Bu Hsien, to rescue him. An angry dispute arose between the two brothers. They started to fight and Mu Chia succumbed. Once more No Chia charged after Li Ching. In his despair Li Ching was about to take his own life when the holy Wen Chiu from the Mount of the Five Dragons, the master of Chin Chia, Li Ching's eldest son, appeared and hid him in his cave. Angrily No Chia demanded that he should surrender him but the holy Wen Chiu said: 'Elsewhere you may give free rein to your nature, but you will not do so in this place.' When No Chia, seething with anger, turned his fiery lance upon him Wen Chiu took a step back, from his sleeve produced the seven-petalled lotus flower and threw it into the air. A whirlwind sprang up, clouds and mist enveloped everything, sand and earth swirled through the air. Then, with a loud crash, everything dropped to the ground. No Chia lost consciousness and when he woke up again he was tied to a golden column with three golden hoops so that he could not move. Wen Chiu now summoned Chin Chia and commanded him to give his misbegotten brother a good thrashing. This he did. No Chia gnashed his teeth but had to submit. At the moment of his supreme trial he saw the Great One approach through the air. He called out to him: 'Master, save me!' The Great One did not listen to him but stepped into the cave and with a smile thanked Wen Chiu for the rough lesson he had administered to No Chia. At last they called him in and commanded him to be reconciled with

35

his father. Then they dismissed the two and sat down to a game of chess. But no sooner was No Chia free again than his anger flared up anew and he resumed his pursuit. Again he had caught up with Li Ching but just then another saint appeared to protect him. This was the ancient Buddha of Glowing Light. When No Chia tried to fight him he raised his sleeve and red swirling clouds turned into a pagoda enclosing No Chia. Glowing Light now placed both his hands on the pagoda. A fire sprang up inside it which burnt No Chia until he cried for mercy. He had to promise to ask his father's forgiveness and to be ever obedient to him. Not until he had made all these pledges did the Buddha release him. He then gave the pagoda to Li Ching and taught him a magic formula with which he could constrain No Chia. Since then Li Ching had been called the pagoda-bearing King of Heaven.

Li Ching and his three sons Chin Chia, Mu Chia and No Chia later helped Emperor Wu of the house of Chou to destroy the tyrant Chou Hsin.

No one could resist their powers. However, a wizard once succeeded in wounding No Chia on his left arm by black magic. Anybody else would have died of the wound. But No Chia was carried by the Great One to his cave. There the Great One treated his wound and gave him three beakers of gods' wine to drink and three fire-dates to eat. When No Chia had eaten and drunk he suddenly heard a loud crack on his left side and a new arm grew from his body. He turned pale with fright, but at that moment another arm grew from his right side. His words stuck in his throat and his eyes started from their sockets with horror. But this was not all: six arms grew from his body and two more heads, so that eventually he had three heads and eight arms. He called out to his master:

'Where is this leading?' but his master laughed and said: 'That's fine! That's fine! Now you will have real power.' Then he taught him the magic of making the arms and heads visible or invisible at will.

When the tyrant Chou Hsin was destroyed Li Ching and his three sons were raised to the rank of gods while still alive and in their earthly bodies.

THE queen of heaven, also called the Holy Mother, in her earthly life was a maiden from Fukien by name of Lin. She was pure, reverent and pious of nature. When she was seventeen she died without having been married. She shows her power at sea, and for that reason she is deeply revered by sailors. Whenever they are unexpectedly assailed by wind and waves they call upon her and she is always ready to answer their prayers.

There are many sailors in Fukien and each year some of them lose their lives. No doubt the queen of heaven, while still on earth, showed pity for the sufferings of her fellow countrymen. And because her mind was ceaselessly concerned with saving the drowning her vision now frequently appears over the sea.

All ships sailing the seas carry a picture of the queen of heaven below deck, as well as three paper talismans. One of these shows her painted with crown and sceptre, another shows her as a maiden in a simple garment, and the third shows her with flowing hair, barefoot, a raised sword in her hand. Whenever a ship is in danger the sailors will burn the first talisman and help will come. If this is not enough they will burn the second and finally the third. If no help has arrived by then the ship is doomed.

Whenever sailors lose their direction in the darkness among the wind and waves they call on the queen of heaven in devout prayer. Thereupon a red light appears on the water. By following that light a ship will safely escape all danger. Frequently also one may see the queen of heaven standing on the clouds, cleaving the wind with her sword. The wind then departs to north and south and the waves are calmed.

The holy picture in a ship always has a wooden stick before it. Sometimes the dragon-fishes of the sea will play with each other. These are two gigantic fishes which pile up the water between them by blowing at it, so that the sun in the sky is darkened and blackness envelops the ocean. From a distance one can often see a bright opening in that darkness. If a ship is then steered straight towards it it will get through and suddenly find itself in calm waters. On looking back one will see the two fishes spewing water. The ship will have passed just beneath their mouths. But a storm is never far away when the dragon fishes are about; that is why some paper or sheep's wool is burned so that the dragons should not drag the ship down into the deep; or else the master of the sticks will burn incense in front of the stick which stands before the holy picture in the cabin. He will pick up the stick and wave it in a circle over the water and the dragons will then draw in their tails and disappear.

Whenever ash flies up in the incense bowl without visible cause and scatters in the air then it is certain that serious danger is threatening.

About two hundred years ago an army was being assembled to conquer Formosa. The general's flag was consecrated with the blood of a white horse. Just then, suddenly, the queen of heaven appeared on top of the flag. An instant later she had disappeared again, but the campaign was successful.

Another time, in the reign of Kien Lung, the minister Chou Ling was ordered to instal a new king on the Ryukyu Islands. As the fleet was sailing past the southern tip

39

of Korea a storm sprang up and the ships were driven far off course into the black vortex. The water looked like ink; sun and moon had lost their brilliance and there was talk among the crew that they were caught in the black vortex whence no man had ever emerged alive. The sailors and passengers lamenting awaited their end. Suddenly a vast number of lights like red lanterns appeared on the surface of the water. The sailors rejoiced and prayed below deck. 'We shall live,' they said, 'the Holy Mother has come.' And indeed a beautiful maiden with golden earrings appeared. She moved her hand through the air and the wind dropped and the waves grew calm. The ship seemed to be drawn by a mighty hand. With a gentle rush it moved through the waves and suddenly it was outside the black vortex.

Chou Ling returned, reported what had happened and requested that a temple be built to the queen of heaven and that she be included in the list of gods. The emperor complied with his request.

Ever since then, temples to the queen of heaven are found in ports everywhere. Her birthday is celebrated with plays and sacrifices on the eighth day of the fourth month.

Nü wa was the sister of Fu Hsi. She helped him with the arranging of marriages. Whereas in the old days men and women had been free to marry whom they chose, Nü Wa ascertained the names of all tribes. Men and women from the same family were no longer allowed to marry. Marriages were concluded by order of the parents. A marriage broker was necessary, and since money did not then exist two skins were laid down as the bridal gift. Thus Nü Wa became known as the divine foundress of marriage, and succeeding generations venerated her as the patroness of matrimony and the guardian of relations between families. After her brother's death she succeeded him on the throne. But a man arose by name of Gung Gung, hirsute of body and with red hair, who considered himself a god because of his wisdom. He occupied the land along the Yangtse and rebelled against the divine princess. He called himself the spirit of the water and used magic formulas to raise a deluge which caused the water to pile up in all the river beds and do great damage to the land.

Nü Wa commanded the Lord of Fire to subdue him. Gung Gung was defeated. In his anger he struck his head against the Mountain of Imperfection and died.

As a result one of the pillars of the sky snapped and the sky tilted towards the north-west. The earth, however, sagged in the region of the new opening in the south-east. Nü Wa thereupon fused some five-coloured stones together with which to mend the sky. She took the legs of a giant turtle and used them as the four poles of the sky.

41

As for the deluge, she channelled it towards the spot where the earth had sunk. That is why to the present day the north-westerly wind is so cold and why all rivers flow towards the south-east to the great sea.

Nü Wa also introduced a system into music. Then she died and temples were built to her.

Once on New Year's Day, the tyrant Chou Hsin of the house of Yin came to the temple of the goddess Nü Wa in order to make a sacrifice there. But a wind sprang up and the curtain in front of the goddess's picture was blown aside. The ruler saw the goddess's golden face. He was inflamed with an unholy love for her, and wrote a poem on the wall and returned home. But the goddess Nü Wa was highly indignant. She commanded the nine-tailed fox to turn into the beautiful girl Ta Chi so as to captivate the ruler and destroy his empire.

Just about that time the tyrant Chou Hsin had issued an order to all his vassals to send the most beautiful girls to him. One of his favourites told him that the Count Su Hu had a daughter by name of Ta Chi whose beauty was matchless. The ruler therefore commanded Su Hu to bring her to him. Su Hu had no choice but to take his daughter to the palace. Halfway there they spent a night at an inn. There the nine-tailed fox caused a magic wind to spring up which carried off Ta Chi's soul. Then he himself entered her body and although he remained a vicious fox the girl's features were unchanged. When the king Chou Hsin caught sight of her he was greatly pleased and she won exceptional favour with him. He would drink wine with her and take his pleasure with her and he ceased to care about the government of the land.

His faithful servants who dared to contradict him were cruelly tortured to death. They were made to embrace red-hot stoves or to walk along narrow greased poles across ditches of blazing fires. In his depravity he no longer knew any bounds to his profligacy. He built a tower which reached up to the stars, he had lakes dug and filled with wine, and he had meat hung up in the forests. Boys and girls were made to chase each other naked, before the eyes of the king and his wife.

One day they were sitting on top of their tower and saw two men, one old and the other young, fording a river. The young man's steps were slow and anxious and he was shivering with the cold, whereas the old man strode out boldly apparently unaware of the cold. The king was astonished but his wife said: 'This is entirely natural. The old one was born at a time when his parents were still young and that is why he has firm marrow in his bones and does not feel the cold. But the young man, born of his parents in their old age, was not equipped with sufficient vigour and that is why his bones are hollow and he feels the cold.' The two were summoned and it was found that the matter of their birth was as Ta Chi had said. But not satisfied with this she had their legs slashed open in order to examine the marrow in their bones. In this manner she committed a thousand cruel deeds.

One day, when the king was reproached by his uncle, Bei Gan, a man universally revered for his wisdom, Ta Chi said: 'I have heard it said that saints and sages have seven openings in their heart. Tear out his heart and let us see whether he is a saint!'

In this manner the tyrant alienated his own relations. The sage Bei Gan, however, was subsequently installed as the god of wealth.

One of the most loyal servants of the ruler was Huang

Fe-hu. He had no equal in wisdom and courage and had earned much renown in war. He urged the ruler not to listen to Ta Chi because he would ruin himself. For that reason Ta Chi hated him deep in her heart. On New Year's Day it was the custom for all the servants of the ruler to call on him with their wives to convey their good wishes. Huang Fe-hu's wife was especially beautiful. Ta Chi therefore hatched a plot. She led her up to the summit of the star tower there to be presented to the king. Secretly, however, she inflamed the king's desire for the woman. Yet the woman resisted all temptations and eventually burst into tears. Thereupon the tyrant grew angry and dragged her by her hair to the edge of the tower and thrust her down from the top so that she was smashed to pieces. When Huang Fe-hu heard about this he was seized with fury; he mounted his five-coloured divine bull which could cover a thousand miles in a day and indignantly left the city. He joined the Emperor Wu who was fighting against the tyrant. But he succumbed to the power of a sorcerer whose wife was familiar with the art of pulling out the sun's rays and turning them into magic needles. She possessed seven times seven such needles and aimed them at the eyes of her husband's enemies. Once they were blinded, her husband then killed them. In this manner Huang Fe-hu lost his life.

When the Emperor Wu had killed the tyrant Chou Hsin and conquered his empire, Huang Fe-hu was proclaimed god of the Great Mountain with power to judge between good and evil, reward and punishment, and life and death for humans, and with power over the ten princes of hell.

13. CONFUCIUS

WHEN Confucius was born a unicorn appeared and spat out a piece of jade on which was written: 'Son of the water crystal, one day you shall be uncrowned king!'

He grew up and was nine feet tall. He had black hair and an ugly face. His eyes protruded and his nose was turned up. His lips did not cover his teeth and his ears had large holes. He studied with great application and was well versed in all things. Thus he became a saint.

One day, with his favourite disciple Yän Hui, he climbed to the highest summit of the Great Mountain. He could see as far as the Yangtse in the south.

'Can you see,' he asked Yän Hui, 'what it is that is glistening outside the city gate of Wu?'

Yän Hui looked closely, strained his eyes, and said: 'It is a piece of white cloth.'

'No,' said Confucius. 'It is a white horse.'

And when they sent someone to find out it really was so. The Great Mountain is a good thousand miles distant from the capital city of Wu and the fact that Confucius was able to make out a white horse at that distance shows his keen-sightedness. Yän Hui could not quite equal him, but at least he saw that there was a white object. That is why he is called the second saint.

Another time a well was being dug in Confucius's native land. In the course of it an animal was discovered which looked like a sheep but only had one leg. No one knew what it was. When they asked Confucius, he said:

'That is a leaping sheep; whenever it appears a great rain will follow.' And sure enough a heavy rain fell soon afterwards.

Another time an object was washed ashore by the Yangtse, and this was green and round and the size of a melon. The King of Chou sent a messenger to ask Confucius what it was. He said: 'The green duck-groat of the Yangtse bears fruit only once every thousand years. Whoever holds this fruit shall have dominion of the world.'

Yet another time a huge bone was dug up in Confucius's native land. The men loaded it on a cart and took it to Confucius to ask him what it was. He said: 'In ancient times the great Yü had summoned the princes of the empire to him. Wind-Keeper alone did not arrive. Yü had him killed and buried at this spot. Wind-Keeper, it is said, was a giant. This is one of his bones.'

When Confucius's death was approaching the Prince of Lu caught a unicorn while out hunting and had it killed. The unicorn which appeared at the time of Confucius's birth had had a red thread tied round its horn by its mother. The dead unicorn now still wore that thread on its horn.

When Confucius heard about this he burst into tears: 'My teaching has been in vain! What is there to be done? I must die.'

The unicorn appears only when a great man lives on earth. At that time Confucius was just writing his book *Of the Rise and Fall of Empires*. When he heard of this occurrence he put down his pen and wrote no more.

He also dreamt he was sitting in a temple between the two central pillars. He said to his disciples: 'Soon I will die.' Then he wrote a song:

The Great Mountain falls,
The roof beam snaps,
The sage departs.

Thereupon he lay down on his bed, fell ill and died.

He therefore not only knew what was happening during his lifetime but also what would befall after his death. The dream of himself in the temple between the two main pillars was a prophecy of the veneration which was to be his due in centuries to come.

But even after his death he gave repeated proof of his omniscience. When the wicked emperor Shih-huang Ti had subjugated all other states and was travelling throughout his empire he came one day to the birthplace of Confucius. There he also saw his tomb. He wanted to have it opened to see what was inside. All his officials advised against it but he would not listen to them. So a passage was dug into it and in the principal chamber a coffin was found. The timber appeared to be entirely fresh. When tapped, it rang like brass. To the left of the coffin was a door which led to an inner chamber. In that chamber, just as if it were inhabited, was a bed, a table with books and clothes. Shih-huang Ti sat down on the bed and looked at the floor. There was a pair of shoes made of crimson silk with a cloud pattern embroidered on their toes. They were new and clean and with no dust on them. Leaning against the wall was a bamboo cane. As a joke the emperor slipped on the shoes, picked up the cane and walked out of the tomb. Suddenly a tablet appeared before him, with the following verse engraved on it:

> Shih-huang Ti overran six lands,
> Opened my tomb and found my bed,
> Stole my shoes, took my staff in his hand,
> Moved on to Sha Chiu—and there dropped dead.

Tsin Shih-huang was terrified and ordered the tomb to be closed up again. But when he reached Sha Chiu he was struck down by a fever and died of it.

Later, during the Han period, when Chung Li-yi was appointed governor of Lu he took ten thousand plummet-weights of his own money and gave it to the guardian of the temple to repair the temple of Confucius. In the course of this work Confucius's cart was discovered, as well as his table, his mat, his sword and his shoes. A temple workman, by name of Chang Bei, who was weeding the grass in front of the great hall, found seven jade sceptres in the ground. He slipped one of them into his pocket and took the others to Chung Li-yi who ordered them to be placed upon Confucius's table. This table used to stand in Confucius's study. Along the wall of the room stood a bed and above the bed there hung a large tun. Chung Li-yi asked the guardian of the temple what it was. He replied: 'It is something left by Confucius. There is an inscription on it; that is why I dared not open it.'

Chung Li-yi said: 'The Master was a saint; perhaps the tun contains the teachings he intended for posterity.'

So the tun was opened. But all it contained was a scrap of paper upon which was written: 'In times to come a sage will arrive and he will put my books in order. He will find my cart and my shoes and my bookcase. Chung Li-yi will receive seven sceptres but Chang Bei will hide one of them.'

48

When Chung Li-yi had read this inscription he summoned Chang Bei and said to him: 'There were seven sceptres here; why did you hide one of them?'

The other man fell on his knees and returned the stolen sceptre to him.

Confucius once said to a disciple: 'The events of a hundred generations can be foretold,' and this story goes to prove it.

KUAN TI, the God of War, was really called Kuan Yü. When the rebellion of the Yellow Turbans swept through the empire he concluded an alliance of friendship with two other men whom he encountered on the road and who, like himself, were fired by patriotism. One of them was the later emperor Liu Bei, the other was called Chang Fei. The three met in a peach orchard and pledged themselves to be brothers to each other even though they came from different families. They slaughtered a white horse and swore loyalty unto death.

Kuan Yü was honest, loyal, just and courageous beyond all measure. He was fond of reading Confucius's book *On the Rise and Fall of Empires*. He helped his friend Liu Bei to suppress the Yellow Turbans and conquer the Four-River Land. The horse he rode was called Red Hare and could cover a thousand miles a day. He had a crescent-shaped knife which was called the Green Dragon. His eyebrows were beautiful like those of silken butterflies and his eyes were slender long slits like those of the phoenix. His face was scarlet and his beard was so long that it reached down to his waist. One day, when he presented himself to the emperor, the emperor called him Duke Fine-Beard and presented him with a silk pouch to keep his beard in. He wore a robe of green brocade. Whenever he went into battle he displayed irresistible courage. No matter whether a thousand armies or ten thousand horsemen were facing him—he regarded them as though they were mere air. Once the wicked Tsau Tsau tempted him to betray his friend and master Liu Bei. Having got Liu Bei's two wives into his power he commanded that Kuan Yü was to be locked up with them in the same room for the night. But Kuan Yü kept his senses and spent the whole night until dawn keeping a vigil on the threshold of the room, a light in his hand.

Another time the wicked Tsau Tsau had encouraged the enemies of Kuan Yü's master to take his city by treachery. As soon as Kuan Yü heard about it he hastened with an army to relieve it. But he ran into an ambush and, together with his son, was taken prisoner and brought to the enemy capital. The ruler of that country would have liked Kuan Yü to join his side, but Kuan Yü swore that he would die rather than yield. Thereupon father and son were executed. After his death his horse, Red Hare, refused all fodder and died. Now Kuan Yü had a loyal captain by name of Chou Tsang, who was black of face and carried a long knife. He had just captured a fortress when he heard of the Duke's tragic end. He drew his sword and killed himself. Another of his faithful followers, upon hearing the news of Kuan Yü's death, threw himself into the city moat and was drowned.

About that time there lived a monk on the Mountain of the Jade Spring, who came from the same part of the country as the Duke and was an old friend of his. He was taking a walk at night, in the moonlight, when suddenly from the air he heard a loud voice crying: 'I want my head back!'

The monk glanced up and saw Duke Kuan mounted on horse-back, a sword in his hand, just as he had been in his life. To the right and left of him were his son Kuan Ping and his General Chou Tsang, like shadows in the clouds.

51

The monk folded his hands and said: 'You were a just man and a loyal one while alive, and now that you are dead you are a wise god—and yet you do not understand destiny? If you insist on having your head back, to whom are those thousands of your enemies to address themselves who met their deaths through you and who likewise want their lives back?'

Upon hearing these words the Duke bowed and vanished.

Since then he has constantly been active as a spirit. Whenever a new dynasty is founded his holy figure appears. For that reason temples have been set up to him and sacrifices made, and he has been included in the number of gods of the empire. Like Confucius he receives great sacrifices of oxen, sheep and pigs. He has risen in rank through the centuries. First he was venerated as the prince Kuan, later as king Kuan, then as a great god who vanquishes the devils, and the last dynasty eventually revered him as a great divine helper of the heavens. He is also known as the war saint and is a powerful saviour in all emergencies, whenever humans are plagued by devils and foxes. He is venerated as the Master of War, together with Confucius, the Master of Peace.

The manifestations of his spiritual powers are beyond number. The following illustration could be multiplied a great many times.

There was a man in Jou Chou who was a drunkard and a gambler and ceaselessly beat and berated his mother. He had a young son who was just a year old. One day the child's grandmother was carrying him in her arms when he made an awkward movement and fell to the ground. The shock he suffered made him ill. The old woman, fearing her son's wrath, ran away from home.

When the son came home and saw that his child was ill he asked his wife how this had come about. At once he rushed out in anger to search for his mother. He caught sight of her outside the temple of the War God, just as she was about to enter it. He snatched her by her hair and dragged her out.

At that the clay statue of the war god in the temple suddenly rose from its seat, snatched the knife from Chou Tsang who was standing behind him, strode out through the door and cut off the man's head. Seeing this, the priest of the temple hurriedly beat the bell and the gong and read from the sacred scrolls. Out in the streets and in the market-place the people heard about the event and came crowding to the temple in amazement. There they saw the War God, the knife in his right hand and in his left the man's head, one foot outside the door and the other inside—thus the statue stood, motionless as a rock. Ever since, the statue of the war god in Jou Chou has been standing there, legs apart, on the threshold of his temple, as evidence of his power.

ALL true gods have a circular halo above their heads. Whenever lesser gods or devils see this halo they cringe and dare not move. The master of heaven on the Dragon Tiger Mountain was well acquainted with all the gods. One day the war god Kuan Yü descended to him just as an official from the neighbouring district was visiting the master of heaven. The master advised the man to withdraw and hide in a back room. He then went to welcome the war god. The official, however, peeped through a crack in the door. He saw the war god's red face and green raiment: he was a terrifying sight which commanded respect. Suddenly on his head a red glow flashed and its rays penetrated to the back room so that the official was blinded in one eye. After a short while the war god left again and the master of heaven went out with him. Just then Kuan Yü said anxiously: 'Confucius is coming! The halo on his head lights up the whole universe. Even I am not his equal at a thousand miles. I will hurry out of his way.' With these words he stepped on a cloud and disappeared. The master of heaven then told the official what had happened, adding: 'Fortunately you did not see the war god eye to eye! Unless a man possesses the highest virtue and the highest knowledge the red glow will melt him.' With these words he gave him a pill of the elixir of life and the man's blind eye gradually improved.

It is also said that sages have a red halo about their heads which is feared by devils, foxes and ghosts.

There was once a sage who had a fox for a friend. The

fox would take him along at night and they would stroll through the villages. They could enter all the houses and see what was happening in them without being noticed by the people. But whenever the fox saw a red glow over a house he would not go in. The sage asked him why.

'These are all famous sages,' the fox replied. 'The brighter the glow the more profound is their wisdom. I shy away from them and dare not enter their houses.'

And the man said: 'Surely I too am a sage. Have I no halo to make you shy away from me?'

'There is only some black mist over your head,' the fox replied. 'Never yet have I noticed a glow there.'

The sage was ashamed and angry, but the fox roared with laughter and made off.

IN point of fact, Lao-tse is older than heaven and earth. He is the Old Yellow Man who, with the other four, created the world. But he appeared on earth at various times under different names. His most famous incarnation is that as the 'old child' (Lao-tse) under the name of Plum (Li). This is how it happened. His mother conceived him in a supernatural way and bore him for 72 years. When he was born he emerged from her left armpit. Moreover, he was able to talk. Since he had no human father he pointed to a plum tree under which he had been born and said: 'That shall be my name!'

He attained great magic skill and with it prolonged his life. One day he hired a servant to work for him. He agreed with him that he would pay him a hundred copper pieces a day; however, he did not pay the man's wages and eventually owed him seven million two hundred thousand copper pieces. He then mounted a black bull and rode off to the west. He wanted to take his servant with him. But when they arrived at the Han Gu pass the servant refused to go any further and demanded his pay. But Lao-tse did not give him anything.

As they approached the house of the guardian of the pass red clouds appeared in the sky. The guardian of the pass understood the sign and knew that a saint was approaching. He walked ahead to meet him and welcomed him to his house. He asked him for some secret wisdom, but Lao-tse stuck out his tongue and said nothing. Nevertheless the guardian of the pass most respectfully invited him to his home. Lao-tse's servant told the guardian's servant that his master owed him a great deal of money and asked him to put in a good word for him. When the servant heard of the large sum he felt tempted to acquire so rich a man for a son-in-law and therefore gave him his daughter for a wife. In the end the guardian of the pass discovered what was going on and, together with the servant, confronted Lao-tse. Then Lao-tse said to his servant: 'You rogue of a servant! You would have long been dead. I hired you, and because I was poor and unable to pay you I gave you a spell of life to eat. That is why you are alive this day. I said to you: If you follow me to the west, to the land of blissful peace, I will pay your wages in yellow gold. But this you did not want!' With these words he slapped the servant's back. The man opened his mouth and out spat the spell of life on to the ground. Upon it one could still read the characters, written with cinnabar, bright as new. But the servant instantly collapsed and turned into a heap of dry bones. The guardian of the pass threw himself to the ground and asked for mercy for the man. He promised to pay the man's wages which Lao-tse owed him and begged him to return the servant to life. Thereupon Lao-tse placed the spell under the bones and instantly the servant revived. The guardian of the pass paid the servant's wages and dismissed him. From then on he revered Lao-tse as his master and Lao-tse imparted to him the secrets of eternal life and left him his teachings in five thousand words which the guardian of the pass wrote down. The book thus written is the book *Of Meaning and Life*. After this, Lao-tse vanished from the eyes of men, but the guardian of the pass followed his teachings and was raised among the immortals.

THERE was once a man named Wang, a young man from an old family who from early youth held the teachings of Taoism in high esteem. He heard that a great many immortals were living in the Lau Shan Mountains. So he humped his box of books on his back and wandered off in that direction.

When he had scaled the summit he caught sight of a lonely temple. A Taoist priest was sitting there on a round bale of straw. His long hair dropped down to his shoulders.

The young man bowed to him and started to speak to him. The priest's words seemed to him profound and mysterious, and he therefore asked to be accepted as a disciple.

The Taoist priest said: 'I am afraid you are too delicate and effeminate for hard work.'

But the young man replied that he could do any work.

The old man had a great many disciples. When they all assembled at nightfall Wang saluted them with solemnity. Thus he was accepted into the monastery.

In the morning, when the air was still cool, the priest called him. He gave him an axe and bade him go out with the others to collect firewood. Wang did eagerly as he was bidden.

A good month had passed. Wang's hands and feet were covered with blisters and callouses. He could hardly bear it any longer and secretly considered returning home.

One evening, on their way back, they saw two men sitting with their master, drinking wine. The sun had set

58

but the lamps and candles had not yet been lit. Thereupon the master took a pair of scissors and from paper cut out a round disc like a mirror. This he stuck to the wall. Suddenly the moon lit up on the wall and was so bright that the finest hair could be distinguished. All the disciples came hastening up to form a circle around the old man and listen to him.

One of the guests said: 'On such a beautiful evening, when joy conquers all, men must be happy together.'

With these words he took up a jug of wine from the table to share it out among the disciples. And he persuaded them to drink deep of it.

Wang said to himself: 'How can one jug of wine be enough for seven or eight persons?' They all hurried to get beakers and jostled to be the first to be served lest the jug be empty before their turn came. But the man poured and poured and the wine still lasted. Wang was amazed but kept silent.

When the second guest said: 'You gave us such beautiful moonlight, but here we are drinking silently to ourselves. How about summoning the moon fairy?'

With these words he took up a chopstick and flung it at the moon disc. And a beautiful young girl came out of the brilliant light. At first she was barely a foot tall but as she touched the ground she grew to human size. Slender hips, a delicate neck, flowing garments—thus she danced the dance of the rainbow. Then she began to sing:

> You all wish to flee, immortals all
> And leave me lonely in this icy hall!

Her voice rang pure and clear like a flute. When she had finished her song she rose, spun round and leapt up

59

on the table. While all eyes were upon her in amazement she once more turned into a chopstick.

The three old men burst into loud laughter.

Then one of the guests again spoke up: 'This is a merry evening indeed. But I am now overcome by the wine. Why don't you accompany me to the moon castle for a parting drink?' So the three now left their mats and slowly moved into the moon. The disciples saw the three men sitting inside the moon. Beard and eyebrows—everything was seen clearly as in a mirror.

After a while the moon gradually grew dim. The disciples went off to fetch lights. When they returned the priest was on his own, the guests had disappeared, but the remains of the food were still on the table. The moon on the wall was no more than a round piece of paper.

The priests asked them: 'Have you had enough to drink?'

They said: 'We've had enough.'

'Well then, if you have had enough you must go to bed early to be fit for your work tomorrow morning.'

Obediently the disciples withdrew. Wang felt encouraged by the evening and his homesickness vanished.

Another month passed. His hardships had become intolerable and the priest had not yet imparted to him a single secret.

In the end he could bear it no longer and took his leave: 'I have come from a hundred miles away to receive wisdom from you. Now I see that I cannot attain the secret of immortality. Still you might have passed on to me something less important, something to satisfy my thirst for knowledge. Two or three months have now gone by without any other occupation than setting out in the morning to gather firewood and coming home tired at night. This is not the kind of life I have been used to.'

The priest said with a smile: 'I told you straight away that you would not be up to the hard work. Now you see that I was right. Tomorrow morning I will discharge you.'

Wang said: 'I served you a long time. You might at least tell me some little trick so I shall not feel I have come here for nothing.'

'And what trick would you like to learn?' the priest asked.

'Watching you I noticed that screens and walls are no obstacles to you. If I but mastered this trick I should be satisfied.'

The priest smilingly agreed and taught him a magic formula with which he must bless himself.

Then he called: 'Now try it!'

Wang was facing the wall but he dared not walk into it.

The priest said: 'Try to walk into it!'

Slowly Wang walked up to the wall but it would not let him through.

The priest said: 'You must bow your head and walk ahead confidently, without fear or hesitation.'

Wang took a few steps back and then ran at the wall. As he came up against it it yielded as though it did not exist. He looked behind him and, true enough, he was outside. He was greatly pleased, walked in again and thanked the priest.

The priest said: 'Well then, go home now! But guard your secret carefully or else it will lose its power.'

Thereupon he gave him food for the journey and dismissed him.

Back home Wang boasted that he had met a saint and

61

that now even the strongest walls no longer presented an obstacle to him. His wife would not believe him. So he wanted to show her his skill, took a few steps back from the wall and ran at it. He hit his head against the hard wall, recoiled and collapsed. His wife picked him up and tended him. On his forehead was a bump the size of an egg. His wife ridiculed him. And he was humiliated and furious and cursed the old priest for being unscrupulous.

ONCE there was a peasant who took his pears to the market. They were very sweet and fragrant and he hoped to get a good price for them. A priest in tattered clothes and torn cap stepped up to his barrow and asked for a pear. The peasant refused him but the priest would not go. Thereupon the peasant got angry and began to berate him. The priest said: 'There are several hundred pears in your barrow. All I ask is one. Surely this is no great loss to you. Why should you get so angry?'

The people around said the peasant should give him a pear and let him go. But the peasant firmly refused. A craftsman in his shop saw what was going on and because the noise annoyed him he took out some money, bought a pear and gave it to the priest.

The priest thanked him and said: 'People like us, who have renounced the world, must not be mean. I myself have beautiful pears and I invite you to eat them with me.' One of the people said: 'If you have pears of your own, why then do you not eat them?' He replied: 'I first need a pip to plant the tree.'

With these words he began to eat the pear, smacking his lips. When he had finished he had a pip in his hand, took the hoe from his shoulder and dug a hole a few inches deep. He placed the pip in it and covered it with earth. Then he asked the people in the market for some soup to water it. A few curious people fetched some hot water from an inn and the priest poured it over the pip. A thousand pairs of eyes were glued to the spot. Presently a

63

shoot sprang up. It grew and grew, and in a moment it had grown to a tree. Branches and leaves developed. The tree blossomed and in no time its first fruit was ripe— masses of big fragrant pears covering the tree. The priest climbed into the tree and handed the pears to those around him. In no time the tree was eaten bare. The priest then took his axe and cut the tree down: chop, chop and it fell. He lifted the tree on to his shoulder and calmly walked away.

While the priest had been practising his magic the peasant had mingled with the spectators. His neck craned forward, his eyes popping, he had stood there, forgetting all about his pears. When the priest had gone he looked for his cart. The pears were all gone. Then he realized that the pears the other man had given away had been his own pears. He looked closer and found the handle of his barrow gone. It had obviously been chopped off recently. The peasant was angry and ran after the priest as fast as he could. But as he turned the corner he saw the missing part of the handle was lying down by the city wall. Then the peasant saw that the pear tree which had been cut down was the handle of his barrow. But the priest was not to be found anywhere. And all the people in the market-place burst out laughing.

ONCE there was a man by name of Wei Bei-yang. He went into the forest with three disciples and there he brewed the elixir of life. Knowing that not all his disciples wholeheartedly believed his teachings, he decided to put them to the test.

He said to them: 'The elixir of life is now ready, but I am not sure of its powers. I will give some to the dog first, to see how it works.'

He gave some to the dog, which died.

Wei Bei-yang thereupon said: 'How difficult it is to get the elixir of life right! I have made it at last, and the dog died of it. It is a sign that I am not destined to attain immortality. Yet I left my wife and child to go into the mountains to learn the secrets of philosophy. I am too ashamed to return home. I would rather die.'

With these words he took some of the elixir of life. No sooner had it touched his lips than he too was dead.

His disciples exchanged frightened glances and said: 'He made the elixir of life, in order to live for ever; instead, he dies of it. What does it mean?'

But one of the disciples said: 'Our master is no ordinary man. Perhaps he only wanted to test our faith.'

So he, too, took some of the elixir of life, but he also died.

Then the other two disciples said to each other: 'This business is uncanny; let's go.'

So they went home to buy coffins for the two dead. The moment they were gone Wei Bei-yang rose up again and also restored his disciple and the little white dog to life. All three entered immortality together. On the way they appeared to the other two disciples. When they saw them they bewailed their foolishness, but it was too late.

ONCE there was a man who was two hundred years old, but he was still youthful and as strong as a young man. His wife bore him a child and when the child was three days old she died. The father gave the child to a neighbour and asked her to look after him. Then he left home and disappeared. As the child was taken to the neighbour's house the first light appeared in the morning sky. For that reason they called him Morning Sky. When the child was three years old he often looked up to the sky and talked to the stars. One day he disappeared and he did not return for many months. The woman beat him. But he left again and did not return for a year. His foster mother was anxious and asked him: 'Where have you been the whole year?' The boy replied: 'I merely ran over to the Purple Sea. The water there made my clothes red. So I went to the source where the sun dwells and washed them clean. I left this morning and it is noon now and I am back. Why are you talking about a year?'

The woman went on asking questions: 'And which way did you go?'

The boy replied: 'After I had washed my clothes I rested a little in the city of the dead and fell asleep. The father king of the East gave me red chestnuts and dawn juice. When I had eaten enough I went to the dark sky and drank some yellow dew to quench my thirst. I then encountered a black tiger and wanted to ride home on his back. But I beat him too hard and he bit me in the leg. That's why I have come back, to tell you all about it.'

Once more the boy ran many thousands of miles away from home, until he came to the swamp where the great primaeval fog hangs. There he encountered a man with yellow eyebrows and asked him his age. The old man said: 'I have given up eating and now live on air. The pupils of my eyes have gradually acquired a green sheen, so I can see all secret things. Every thousand years I turn my bones and rinse their marrow. Every two thousand years I scrape my skin and get rid of the hairs. I have washed my marrow three times and scraped my skin five times.'

Morning Sky later served the emperor Wu of the Han dynasty. The emperor, who was very fond of magic, made him his favourite. One day he said to him: 'I would like my favourite wife to stay young. Is that possible?'

Morning Sky replied: 'I alone know the secret of staying young.'

The emperor asked what herbs would have to be eaten. Morning Sky replied: 'The mushroom of life grows in the north-east. The three-legged crow in the sun is always anxious to fly down and eat of it. But the sun god holds the bird's eyes covered and does not let it go. When humans eat of it they become immortal, if animals eat of it they are stunned.'

'How do you know all this?' asked the emperor.

'As a boy I once fell into a deep well and could not get out for many decades. There was an immortal who led me to this mushroom. But to get there one has to cross the Red Water and that is too weak even to support a floating feather. Anything that touches it sinks to the bottom. But that man took off his shoe and gave it to me. In the shoe I sailed across the water, picked the mushroom and ate it. The people in that place weave mats

68

from pearls and precious stones. They took me into a room which had a curtain of a thin brilliantly coloured skin. They gave me a cushion carved from black jade with sun and moon, clouds and thunder engraved into it. They covered me with a fine blanket which was woven of the hair of a hundred mosquitos. That blanket was quite cool and very refreshing in the summer. I touched it with my hand and it seemed to me to consist of water, but when I looked closer I could see it was all light.'

One day the emperor summoned all his learned men to talk to them about the fields of the blessed. Morning Sky was also present and told them: 'Once while wandering about the North Pole I came to the Fire Mirror Mountain. There, neither sun nor moon stands in the sky. But there is a dragon with a fiery mirror in his jaws to lighten the darkness. On the mountain is a park and in the park a lake. By the lake grows the grass with the gleaming blades, brilliant like a golden lamp. If one picks it and uses it as a candle one can see not only all things visible but also the shapes of ghosts. Even the inside of humans can be seen by its light.'

One day Morning Sky went to the east, to the country of the clouds of fortune. From there he brought back the horse of the gods. The horse was nine feet tall. The emperor asked how he had found it.

Morning Sky related: 'The Western Mother had hitched it to her carriage when she went to visit the father king of the east. The horse was tethered in the field of the mushrooms of life. But he trampled down several hundreds of them. Thereupon the father king got angry and drove the horse towards the river of heaven. There I found him and rode him back home. Three times I circled the sun because I had fallen asleep on horseback.

And before I knew it I was here. This horse can overtake the shadow of the sun. When I found him he was as thin and sorrowful as an old donkey. But I mowed the grass in the country of the clouds of fortune by the mountain of the nine springs, where it only grows once every two thousands years, and fed it to the horse and he soon recovered his spirits.'

The emperor asked him about the country of the clouds of fortune.

Morning Sky replied: 'There is a big swamp there. The people predict fortune and misfortune from the air and the clouds. If good fortune is to befall a house then five-coloured clouds will form in the rooms and they will settle on grass and trees, turning into coloured dew. That dew tastes as sweet as must.'

The emperor asked if he might have some of that dew. Morning Sky replied: 'On my horse I can get there and back four times in a day.'

And true enough he was back by nightfall with some many-coloured dew in a crystal bottle. The emperor drank of it and his hair turned black again. He gave some of it to his highest officials and the old men were young again and the sick were cured.

Once, when a comet appeared in the sky, Morning Sky handed the emperor the astrologer's rod. The emperor pointed it at the comet and the comet was extinguished.

Morning Sky played the flute beautifully. Whenever he played his rich drawn-out notes the grains of sun-dust danced to his tune.

One day he said to a friend: 'No man except the astrologer knows who I am.'

When Morning Sky died the emperor called the

70

astrologer and asked him: 'Did you know Morning Sky?'

The man said: 'No.'

The emperor asked: 'What is your skill?'

The astrologer said: 'I observe the stars.'

'Are all the stars in their places?' asked the emperor.

'Yes. But for eighteen years I had not seen the Star of the Great Year. Now it has appeared again.'

Thereupon the emperor looked up at the sky and heaved a sigh: 'For eighteen years Morning Sky was at my side and I never knew that he was the Star of the Great Year.'

IN the days of King Mu of Chou a magician came from the far west who knew how to pass through fire and water, penetrate metal and stone, move mountains and rivers, shift cities and castles, step into the void without falling and encounter solid obstacles without being held up by them. He knew an inexhaustible number of transformations. He could change not only the shape of things but also men's thoughts. The king revered him like a god and served him as a servant does his master. He gave up his own apartments to accommodate the magician, he had sacrificial animals brought to him, and he chose girl singers for his delight. But the magician found the apartments in the king's castle too poor to live in, the food from the king's kitchen too evil-smelling to feast on and the girls of the royal harem too ugly to touch. King Mu therefore had a new palace built for the magician. The work of masons and carpenters, of painters and decorators left nothing to be desired in its skill. The treasury was empty when the tower reached its full height. It was a thousand ells high and stood higher than the summit of the mountain outside the capital. The king chose the most beautiful and delicate virgins, supplied them with perfumes, had their eyebrows drawn in beautiful lines and adorned them with hair ornaments and ear pendants. He clothed them in fine cloth and wrapped them in soft silks, he had their faces painted white and their eyebrows black, he put bangles of precious stones on their arms and made them blend fragrant herbs. He filled the palace with them and they sang the songs of the ancient kings to please the magician. Every month the most precious clothes were brought to him and each morning the most delicious meals. The magician was well pleased, and as he could do no better for himself he took what was offered.

Some time later he invited the king to accompany him on a journey. The king held on to the magician's sleeve. Thus they soared up right into the sky. When they stopped they were at the magician's castle which was built of gold and silver and adorned with pearls and precious stones. It towered above clouds and rain; no man knew upon what it rested. To the eye it seemed like clouds piled upon one another. Whatever the senses perceived was altogether different from things in the human world. The king felt as though he had been transported to the purple depths of the city of the ether, amidst the harmony of the spheres of heaven, where the great god dwelt. The king glanced down and saw his own castles and pleasure palaces like mounds of earth and piles of straw. For a few decades the king dwelt there and no longer thought of his empire.

Then the magician again invited the king to travel with him. At the place they came to they saw neither sun nor moon above them, nor rivers nor sea below them. The king's eyes were too blinded with light for him to recognize the shapes about him; his ears were too deafened to perceive the sounds which fell upon them. His whole body seemed to dissolve in confusion, his thoughts were disturbed and he was about to lose consciousness. He asked the magician to allow him to return. The magician put a spell on him and the king thought he was falling into emptiness.

When he came to he was sitting in the same place as

73

before. The attendant servants were the same as before. The king glanced up and his beaker was not yet empty nor his food cold.

The king asked what had happened. The servants replied: 'The king sat in silence for a short while.' This so upset the king that it was three months before he recovered. He then questioned the magician. The magician said to him: 'I travelled with you in spirit, oh king— what need is there for the body to move? The places we dwelt in were no less real than your castle and your gardens. You are used only to permanent states, that is why you find suddenly dissolving apparitions so strange.'

The king was happy enough. He no longer cared about affairs of state, he took no pleasure in his servants or women but decided to go on a long journey. He commanded the eight famous horses to be harnessed and with a few faithful followers travelled a thousand miles. He came to the country of the great hunters. These brought the king the blood of the snow-goose to drink and washed his feet in the milk of horses and cattle. When they had drunk they continued their journey and spent the night on the slope of the K'unlun Mountain to the south of the Red Water. The following day they climbed to the summit of the K'unlun Mountain and looked towards the castle of the lord of the Yellow Earth. Then they travelled on to the mother who is queen in the west. Before getting there they had to cross the weak water, which is a river whose waves are not buoyant enough to bear rafts or ships. Whatever crosses this water sinks to the bottom. But as the king reached the bank fishes and turtles, crabs and newts came swimming up and formed a bridge so that the king's carriage could drive across.

It is said that the mother who is queen in the west has

tangled hair, a bird's beak and tiger's fangs and that she is skilled at flute playing. However, that is not her true shape but only an attendant spirit which looks after the western sky. The mother queen welcomed king Mu at her castle by the jasper spring. She gave him rock marrow to drink and the fruits of the jasper tree to eat. Then she sang a song to him and taught him a spell which ensures long life. The mother who is queen in the west gathers around her the immortals whom she feasts with the peaches of long life; they arrive in carriages with purple canopies, drawn by flying dragons. Ordinary mortals sink in the weak water as they try to cross it. But she was favourably disposed towards king Mu.

When he left her he passed the place where the sun dwells after driving three thousand miles a day. Then he returned to his empire. When he was a hundred years old the mother who is queen in the west arrived at his palace and carried him up with her among the clouds.

Since that day he has not been seen again.

ONCE there was a man who was known as old Chiang. He lived in the country near Yangchow as a gardener. His neighbour, called Wei, was an official in Yangchow, whose daughter had just reached marriageable age. He therefore summoned a marriage broker and instructed her to find a handsome bridegroom. When old Chiang heard about this he was greatly pleased. He prepared food and wine, invited the marriage broker and told her to recommend him as a bridegroom. But the old woman left him, scolding and ranting.

The following day he again invited her and gave her money. The old woman said: 'You do not know what you are asking. Why should the beautiful daughter of a great gentleman marry a poor old gardener? Even if you had pots of money your white hair and thin blood would not suit her. There can be no question of marriage.'

But old Chiang persisted, urging her: 'Just try and mention my name! If they do not listen to you then I shall have to bear my fate.'

The old woman had accepted his money and therefore, even though she was afraid of being rebuked, suggested him to the lord Wei. But he got angry and wanted to throw her out.

'I knew you would blame me,' the old woman said, 'but the old man so pestered me I could not help telling you of his intentions.'

'Tell the old man he can have my daughter for a wife if he brings me this very day two lumps of white jasper and four hundred plummet-weights of yellow gold.'

But he merely intended to mock the old man's foolishness, for he knew that he could never produce such riches. The woman went to see old Chiang and gave him the message. Old Chiang agreed and instantly took the full amount of gold and the precious stones to the house of the lord Wei. Wei was greatly startled and his wife, when she heard the news, began to lament and wail. But the girl comforted her mother: 'My father has given his word and I must not break it. I know how to bear my fate.'

So the lord Wei gave his daughter to old Chiang. Chiang did not give up gardening even after his marriage. He still carted manure, hoed his field and sold his vegetables as before. His wife had to carry water and make the fire in her kitchen. All this she did without being ashamed. Her relations rebuked her but she remained steadfast.

One day a noble relation came to see the lord Wei and said to him: 'Even if you are poor surely there were enough young gentlemen in the neighbourhood for your daughter. Why did you have to let her marry such an old wrinkled gardener? Now that you have thrown her away like that it would be better if the two left the neighbourhood.'

Then the lord Wei prepared a banquet and invited his daughter and old Chiang to his house. When they had drunk a good deal of wine he hinted at what he wanted.

Old Chiang said: 'I only stayed here because I thought you would miss your daughter. But if you are tired of us I will gladly move away. I have a small country house beyond the mountains. Early tomorrow we shall depart.'

The next morning, just at daybreak, old Chiang and his wife came to say goodbye. The lord Wei said: 'If we should miss you later my son can go out and look you up.' Old Chiang put his wife on a donkey and put a straw hat on her head. He himself picked up a stick and walked behind.

A few years passed without any news from the two. The lord Wei and his wife missed their daughter and sent out their son to enquire about her. When he had arrived on the far side of the mountains he came upon a servant ploughing with a team of yellow bullocks. He asked him : 'Where is the country house of old Chiang?'

The servant let go of the plough, bowed and said: 'You have been a long time coming, master. The village is not far from here. I will show you the way.'

They crossed another mountain. At its foot ran a stream. Having forded the stream they had to climb another mountain. Gradually the scenery changed. From the summit they could see a valley, flat in the middle, surrounded by steep peaks and shaded by green trees from among which peered roofs and turrets. That was the country house of old Chiang. Outside the village ran a deep stream with clear blue water. They crossed a stone bridge and reached the gate. There were thick clumps of trees and flowers. Peacocks and cranes fluttered about. From afar came the sound of flutes and strings. The pure notes rose up to the clouds. A herald in purple attire received the guest at the gate and led him into a hall which was splendid in the extreme. The air was filled with strange perfumes and with the tinkle of pearly bells. Two women servants came out to welcome him. They were followed by two long rows of beautiful girls. Behind them came a man with a soft turban, robed in scarlet silk and wearing red slippers on his feet. The guest saluted him. He was solemn and dignified and yet youthfully vigorous. At first he did not recognize him, but as he looked closer he saw that he was old Chiang. With a smile Chiang said: 'I am glad the long journey did not deter you. Your sister is just combing her hair. She will receive you in a moment.' Then he invited him to sit down and drink tea.

After a little while a serving maid came and led him to the inner rooms of his sister. The beams of her room were of sandal-wood, the doors were made of tortoise-shell, the windows were encrusted with blue jasper, the curtains were strings of pearls and the steps were of green jade. His sister was magnificently arrayed and far more beautiful than before. She asked him lightly how he was and how their parents were, but she was not particularly cordial. After a superb repast they prepared a room for him.

'My sister would like to take your sister on an excursion to the Fair Mountain,' old Chiang said to him. 'We shall be back by sunset. You may rest here until we get back.'

Thereupon brightly coloured clouds rose up in the court-yard and delightful music rang out. Old Chiang mounted a dragon, his wife and his sister rode on phoenixes, and their entourage on cranes. Thus they rose up into the air and disappeared in the east. They did not return till after sunset.

Old Chiang and his wife said to him: 'This is a house of the blessed. You may not stay here too long. Tomorrow we shall see you off.'

The following day, as they parted, old Chiang gave him eighty plummet-weights of gold and an old straw hat. 'Whenever you need money,' he said to him, 'you can go to Yangchow and ask for old Wang's pharmacy in the northern suburb. There you can draw ten million copper pieces. This hat is your voucher for them.' Then he commanded the servant to accompany him home.

Back home, when the brother reported what he had seen, many thought that old Chiang was a saint, but others believed it had all been a magic illusion.

After five or six years the lord Wei's money had run out. His son therefore went to Yangchow with the straw hat and there asked for old Wang. Wang was just standing outside his pharmacy, blending herbs. When he heard the request he said: 'The money is here. But is this hat genuine?' He took the hat in his hands and looked at it closely. From an inner room a young girl came out and said: 'I myself wove the hat for old Chiang; there should be a red thread in it.' And true enough there was. So Wang gave the ten million copper pieces to Yang Wei, and Yang Wei now really believed old Chiang to be a saint. He therefore once more crossed the mountains to see him. When he came to the summit the path had disappeared. He questioned some woodcutters but they knew nothing. Sadly he turned back. He wanted to question old Wang, but he had vanished too.

Several years later he was in Yangchow again and was walking in the meadow outside the gate. There he came upon the servant of old Chiang. The servant asked him: 'And how are things with you?' and produced ten pounds of yellow gold from his pocket. He gave them to him and said: 'My mistress commanded me to give this to you. My master is just drinking wine with old Wang in the inn across the road.' He followed the servant and wanted to greet his brother-in-law. But when he came to the inn there was no one to be seen there. He turned about and the servant too had disappeared. Old Chiang has never been heard of since.

80

ONCE there was a man by name of Tu Chih-chun. He was a spendthrift in his youth and did not look after his fortune. He indulged in wine and drifted about all day long. When he had spent all he owned his family cast him out. One day during the bitter winter he was walking about the capital barefoot, with an empty stomach, his clothes in rags. Evening was falling and he had still not eaten anything. Aimlessly he wandered about the market-place. He was hungry and the cold seemed unbearable. He glanced up at the sky and lamented bitterly.

Suddenly an old man stood before him, supporting himself on a staff, and said: 'What is the matter with you, why do you lament so?'

'I am dying of hunger,' said Tu Chih-chun, 'and nobody has pity on me.'

The old man asked: 'How much money do you need in order to live well?'

'If I had fifty thousand copper pieces my troubles would be over,' replied Tu Chih-chun.

The old man said: 'That's not enough.'

'Well then, a million.'

'Even that is not enough.'

'Three million, then.'

The old man said: 'Very well!' He produced a thousand copper pieces from his sleeve and said: 'This is for tonight. Wait for me in the Persian bazaar at noon tomorrow!'

At the appointed time Tu Chih-chun went to the bazaar and, true enough, the old man was there and gave him

81

three million copper pieces. He then disappeared without giving his name.

As soon as Tu Chih-chun had all that money in his hand his extravagance awoke in him anew. He rode about on fat horses, clothed himself in the finest furs, got drunk on wine and was forever surrounded by singing girls. Thus the money was soon spent. Instead of his fine brocades he had to wear cotton clothes and exchange his horse for a donkey. Before very long he was once more in rags, on foot, wondering how to appease his hunger. Once again he stood in the market-place sighing.

And again the old man appeared, took him by the hand and said: 'Have you come to the same pass again? How strange! I will help you once more.'

Tu Chih-chun was ashamed and did not want to accept. But the old man insisted and took him along to the Persian bazaar. There he gave him ten million copper pieces this time, and Tu Chih-chun, deeply ashamed, thanked him.

Now that he had the money he was careful to account and economize in order to become as rich as possible. But deeply ingrained faults, as everybody knows, are difficult to eradicate. Gradually he started squandering his money again and giving free rein to his appetites. And once more his purse was empty. After a year or two he was as poor as ever.

Again he met the old man. He was so ashamed that he hid his face and tried to walk past him.

But the old man caught him by the sleeve and said: 'Where do you think you are going? I will give you thirty million this time. But if you still do not mend your ways then there is no help for you.' Gratefully Tu Chih-chun bowed and said: 'None of my rich relations cared about me while I was poor. You alone have helped me three times. The money which you are giving me today shall not be squandered—that I swear to you. I want to use it for good works in order to reward your great kindness. And when I have achieved this I will follow you, even through fire and water.'

The old man said: 'Well spoken! When you have settled these matters ask for me at the temple of Lao-tse under the two juniper trees.'

Tu Chih-chun took the money and went to Yangchow. There he bought a hundred acres of the best land and built a tall house on the highway with many hundreds of rooms. There he allowed widows and orphans to live. He then bought a burial ground for his ancestors and supported his needy relations. Countless people owed their livelihood to him.

When he had done all this he went out to find the old man at the temple of Lao-tse. The old man was sitting in the shade of the juniper trees, playing his flute. He now took him along to the cloud-capped summit of the holy mountain in the west. They had walked through the mountains for forty miles when Tu Chih-chun caught sight of a house which was neat and beautiful. It was surrounded by brightly coloured clouds, and peacocks and cranes flew around it. Inside the house was a herb oven which was nine feet high. The fire in it burned with a purple flame and its glow danced on the walls. There were nine fairies standing by the oven, and a green dragon and a white tiger were crouched alongside. Night was falling. The old man was no longer arrayed as an ordinary human but wore a yellow cap and loose flowing garments. He picked up three white stone balls, put them in a beaker of wine and gave them to Tu Chih-chun to drink. He spread out a tiger skin in an inner room along the western

83

wall and made him sit down on it with his face to the east. Then he spoke to him: 'Be careful now not to utter a single word! Whatever happens to you—powerful gods or hideous devils, wild animals or ogres, all the torments of hell, and even if you see your own relations in pain and suffering, all these are but illusions. You have nothing to fear. They cannot hurt you. Mark my words and be of good cheer!' With these words the old man disappeared.

All Tu Chih-chun saw before him now was a large stone jug full of clear water. The fairies, the dragon and the tiger had all disappeared. Suddenly he heard a loud crash which shook heaven and earth. A man appeared, over ten feet tall. He called himself the great general. Both he and his horse were in golden armour. He was surrounded by over a hundred soldiers who pulled their bow-strings and swung their swords as they halted in the courtyard.

The giant shouted at him: 'Who are you? Get out of my way!'

But Tu Chih-chun did not budge. He made no reply to the giant's questions.

Then the giant was furious and screamed with a voice of thunder: 'Cut off his head!'

But Tu Chih-chun remained unmoved. Thereupon the giant angrily moved off.

Then came a wild tiger and a poisonous snake, roaring and hissing. They moved up to him as though to bite him and leapt over him. But Tu Chih-chun remained unshaken in his spirit and after a while they dissolved.

Suddenly a great rain burst from the sky. There was ceaseless thunder and lightning until his ears rang and his eyes were blinded. The house seemed certain to collapse. In a few moments the water rose and reached the spot where he was sitting. But Tu Chih-chun remained motion-less and paid no heed. So the water receded.

Then came a great devil with the head of an ox. He placed a cauldron in the courtyard and in it bubbled boil-ing oil. With an iron hook he caught Tu Chih-chun by the neck and said: 'If you tell your name I will let you go!'

Tu Chih-chun closed his eyes and remained silent. Thereupon the devil with the fork tossed him into the cauldron. He bit back the pain and the boiling oil did him no harm. In the end the devil fished him out again and dragged him to the front steps of a house where there was a man with red hair and a blue face who looked like the Prince of Hell himself. He screamed: 'Drag his wife here!'

After a while Tu Chih-chun's wife was brought in fetters. Her hair was dishevelled and she was crying piti-fully.

The devil pointed to Tu Chih-chun and said: 'If you tell us your name we'll let you go.'

But Tu Chih-chun did not utter a word.

Then the Prince of Hell had the woman tormented in all kinds of ways. Tu Chih-chun's wife implored him: 'I have been living with you for ten years. Won't you say a single word to save me? I can bear it no longer!' And the tears burst from her eyes in streams. She cried and scolded him. But he uttered not a word.

Then the Prince of Hell shouted: 'Hack her into pieces!' And true enough she was cut into pieces in front of his eyes, moaning and screaming. But Tu Chih-chun did not budge.

'This rascal's measure is full!' shouted the Prince of Hell. 'He cannot remain among the living any longer. Cut off his head!'

They killed him and he felt his soul departing. The one with the ox head now dragged him into a cave where he had to submit to each and every torment. But Tu Chih-chun heeded the words of the old man. Even these torments did not seem unbearable. He did not scream and did not utter a word.

He was dragged back before the Prince of Hell. He said: 'As a punishment for his obduracy this man shall be reborn a woman.'

The devils dragged him to the wheel of life and he was reborn on earth as a girl. He was frequently ill and had to take medicine all the time or be treated by pinpricks and burning. Moreover, he often fell into the fire or the water. But he never uttered a single sound. Gradually he grew up to be a beautiful young girl. But because he never uttered a word he was called the mute girl. A scholar fell in love with her beauty and married her. They lived in love and harmony and she bore him a son who, even at the age of two, was clever and wise beyond all measure.

One day the father carried him on his arm. Then he joked with his wife: 'Sometimes when I look at you it seems to me as though you were not mute. Won't you say a single word to me? How delightful it would be if you were to be my speaking rose!'

But the woman remained silent. No matter how much he flattered her and tried to make her laugh she never made any reply.

Then his expression changed: 'If you will not speak to me,' he said, 'I take this as a sign that you despise me. In that case my son is no use to me.' With these words he seized the boy and struck his head against a stone so that his brains squirted out.

But because Tu Chih-chun loved the young boy he forgot the old man's injunctions and exclaimed: 'Oh, oh!'

And before the sound had even died away he awoke, as though from a dream, sitting in his former place. The old man, too, was present. It was about the fifth watch of the night. From the oven the purple flames flickered wildly, their tongues licking the sky. The whole house caught fire and blazed like a torch.

'You have let me down!' the old man exclaimed. Then he took him by the hair and thrust him into the water jug. And in an instant the fire was extinguished. The old man said: 'You conquered joy and anger, sadness and fear, hatred and lust—but you did not extinguish love. If you had not called out as the child was killed my elixir would have come right and you too would have attained immortality. But at the last moment you failed. Now it is too late. Now I must brew my elixir all over again and you will remain a mortal.'

Tu Chih-chun saw that the stove had burst and that instead of the philosopher's stone there was a lump of pig-iron in it. The old man threw off his clothes and hacked the iron into small pieces with a magic knife. Tu Chih-chun took his leave and returned to Yangchow where he lived in great wealth.

In his old age he regretted not having finished his task at the time. He went back to the mountain to look for the old man. But he had vanished without a trace.

MU LIEN was a famous Buddhist in the Tang dynasty. He entered a monastery as a young man, awakened to the understanding of the mind and became a Buddha. But his mother was rude and envious of nature. She despised the gifts of god, trampled bread under foot and allowed remnants of food to lie about her floor. And whenever a beggar came and asked for some food she ignored him. In later years she developed difficulties in swallowing and had to suffer hunger for many days. Then she died. Two devils dragged her away. The way to the beyond led over the mountain of deeds and the river of the underworld, and the devils tormented her in every possible manner. When she arrived in the underworld the god of the dead was very angry and ordered her to be locked up in the hell of hunger. Hunger made her insides grumble like thunder but she was not given a single grain to eat. Whenever she cried out with hunger all the hungry spirits joined in. Therefore the wardens pinned her tongue down with an iron awl so she could not utter a sound, and they lit two lamps in front of her eyes so she could not see anything. She would have preferred to die all over again, but she was not granted that favour.

At that time Mu Lien had reached the grade of Buddha. He knew that his mother was dead. So he descended to the underworld and stepped before the god of the dead. He wanted to bring his mother an alms dish of rice. The ruler of the dead gave him permission but warned him: 'I fear she will want to eat but will not be able to do so.

None can escape the punishment they have brought upon themselves.'

Mu Lien went to the hell of hunger and demanded to see his mother. The wardens extinguished the lamps in front of her eyes and released her tongue. When Mu Lien saw his mother he threw himself down before her, sobbing, and his mother, too, cried and said: 'I am very hungry.' Mu Lien brought her his alms dish. But as she tried to swallow the food the fire inside her flashed out through her mouth so she could not eat anything. Thereupon the wardens dragged her back into hell and locked the door upon her.

Mu Lien was bitterly angry and with all his strength struck the prison door with his iron rod until it burst open. Then he took his mother on his back and carried her up into heaven. But hundreds and thousands of hungry devils pushed out behind him and scattered in all directions and sneaked back into life. The god of the dead did not dare oppose the boundless power of a Buddha but he got the god of the great mountain to report the affair to the Lord of Heaven. The Lord of Heaven decided: 'Mu Lien saved his mother; this shows a praiseworthy filial mind. His mother therefore shall be pardoned. But he also allowed all the locked-up criminals to escape and bring disaster to living men. For that reason Mu Lien must go back to earth to round up all those hungry devils and get them back to hell. Only then will he be readmitted to heaven.'

Towards the end of the Tang dynasty the Huangchow rebellion broke out in which many hundreds of thousands lost their lives. Those were the hungry devils who had sneaked back into the world. But Huangchow was Mu Lien who in this manner discharged his task.

89

ONCE there was a scholar who had retired from the world to discover the secrets of life. He lived alone in a remote spot. All round his small house he had planted flowers, bamboos and trees, until it was entirely hidden in a thick clump of blossoms. He had a single boy servant who lived in a separate hut and waited upon his master's orders, and who was not allowed to enter unbidden. The scholar loved flowers above everything else, but he never went outside the boundaries of his garden.

One fine spring evening, when the trees were in blossom and the flowers in full bloom, when a gentle wind was blowing and the moon shining brightly, he sat over a cup of wine, enjoying life.

Suddenly in the light of the moon he saw a graceful girl in dark attire approach him. She bowed deeply, saluted him and said: 'I am your neighbour. There is a company of girls outside who are travelling to visit their eighteen aunts. They would like to rest a little in your courtyard and have sent me to ask your permission.'

The scholar realized that this was something out of the ordinary and therefore he consented gladly. The girl thanked him and left. After a short while she brought back with her a whole crowd of girls carrying flowers and willow switches, who all greeted the scholar. They were pretty with fine faces and slim graceful figures, and whenever they moved their sleeves they emitted a delightful perfume. They had no equal in the human world.

The scholar invited them to come in and sit down. Then

90

he asked them: 'By whom am I honoured? Have you come from the palace of the moon fairy or from the jade spring of the mother queen of the west?'

'How could we boast of such exalted origin?' a girl in a green robe asked with a smile. 'My name is Salix.' Then she introduced another girl, dressed in white, and said: 'This is Miss Prunophora,' and one dressed in pink: 'And here is Persica,' and finally one in a brilliant red garment: 'And this is Punica. We are all sisters and intend to visit our eighteen zephyr aunts today. This evening the moon is so beautiful and this garden here is so lovely. We are indeed grateful to you for your hospitality.'

'Yes, indeed,' said the scholar.

Suddenly the servant in the dark robe came in and announced: 'The zephyr aunts have also arrived.'

Instantly the girls got up and went to the door to meet them.

'We are just on our way to visit the aunts,' they said with a smile. 'This gentleman here has invited us to sit down for a while. How pleasant to find that the aunts have come here as well. Tonight is such a beautiful night; we really must drink to the health of our aunts.'

Thereupon they commanded the servant girl to bring in what was necessary.

'May we take a seat?' the aunts asked.

'The master of this house is very kind,' the girls replied, 'and this place is quiet and remote.'

Thereupon they introduced the scholar to the aunts. He said a few friendly words to the eighteen aunts. There was something airy and unstable about them. Their words came rushing out and, sitting near them, their breath felt chilly.

Meanwhile the servant girl had carried in a table and

chairs. The eighteen aunts sat at the head of the table. Then came the girls, and the scholar sat down by them in the lowest place. In an instant the whole table was covered with the most delicious food and the most wonderful fruit, and the cups were full of fragrant wine, more delightful than any in the human world. The moon was shining brightly and the flowers gave out an intoxicating scent. When the wine had made them merry, the girls got up and danced and sang. The notes floated delightfully through the dark night and their dance was like that of butterflies hovering over flowers. Enraptured, the scholar no longer knew whether he was in heaven or on earth.

When the dance was at an end the girls sat down at the table again and let their cups circle to the health of the aunts. There was also a toast to the scholar and he replied in elegant words.

But the eighteen aunts were a little frivolous in their nature. The wine, moreover was beginning to affect them. And as one of them raised her cup her hand shook a little and before she knew it she had spilt some of her wine on Punica's clothes. Punica, who was young and fiery and loved cleanliness, rose angrily as she saw her red robe stained with wine.

'You are too careless,' she said angrily. 'The other sisters are afraid of you, but I have no fear of you.'

Thereupon the aunts for their part became angry and said: 'How dare that young thing be rude to us!'

With these words they gathered up their robes and rose to their feet.

All the girls crowded around them and said: 'Punica is young and inexperienced. She is drunk and does not know what she is doing. You must not blame her. Tomorrow she shall call on you with a switch and receive her punishment.'

But the eighteen aunts would not listen to them and left. Thereupon the girls also took their leave, dispersed among the flowerbeds and disappeared. For a long time the scholar sat lost in a nostalgic dream.

The following evening the girls all came again.

'We all live in your garden,' they told him. 'Each year we are plagued by evil winds and that is why we have always asked our eighteen aunts to protect us. Yesterday Punica offended them and we are afraid that they will not help us in future. But we know that you have always been fond of us sisters and for that we are deeply grateful to you. We now have a great request—each New Year's Day you shall make a small scarlet flag and paint on it the sun, the moon and the five planets and plant it at the eastern end of the garden. Then we sisters shall have peace and be protected against all suffering. But since the New Year is now past we ask you to put up the flag on the twenty-first of this month; that is when the east wind comes, but the flag will protect us.'

The scholar readily promised to do as they asked and the girls said with one voice: 'We thank you for your great kindness and will repay you.' With these words they left him and a sweet fragrance hung over the whole garden.

The scholar then made just such a red flag and early in the morning of the appointed day, when the east wind in fact started to blow, he quickly planted it in the garden.

Abruptly a fierce storm broke, making the forests bow low and snapping the trees. But in the garden the flowers did not move at all.

Then the scholar discovered that Salix was the willow,

Prunophora the plum, Persica the peach, and the young outspoken Punica the pomegranate, and the wind was powerless against their vigorous blossoms. But the eighteen zephyr aunts were the spirits of the wind.

The following evening the flower fairies again all arrived and in gratitude brought him a bunch of brilliant flowers.

'You have saved us,' they said. 'We have nothing else that we can give you. But if you eat these flowers you will live many long years without growing old. And if you protect us each year then we sisters too will have a long life.'

The scholar did as he was told and ate the flowers. Instantly his appearance changed and he was as young as a man of twenty. In the course of time he discovered the secrets of life and was translated among the immortals.

To the west of Kiauchou Bay is the Wulien mountain, the home of many ghosts. Once there was a scholar who lived nearby, and one night he stayed awake until late, reading. When he stepped outside his house a storm suddenly sprang up and a monster reached out its claws for him and seized him by the hair. It lifted him up into the air and carried him away. It carried him past the Watchtower of the Sea, which is a Buddhist temple in the mountains. There, from afar, he saw in the clouds the figure of a god in golden armour. The figure was just like the image of Wei To which was on the tower. In its right hand it held an iron club and its left hand pointed at the monster with an angry gesture. At once the monster let the scholar drop, right on to the top of the tower, and then vanished. No doubt the saint in the tower had come to his help because his whole family devoutly revered the Buddha.

When the sun rose the priest arrived and saw him on his tower. He piled up hay and straw on the ground, so the scholar could jump down without injuring himself. He was taken back home, but at the places where the monster had seized him his hair remained stiff and inflexible. Not until six months later did it begin to heal.

THERE is a village at the foot of the Horse Mountain. In that village there dwelt a peasant who made his living by selling grain. Every five days he would go to the small market town east of the village. This market was about a mile away and separated from the village by a rocky ridge.

One day he was returning from the market slightly drunk. He was on his mule and had just reached the rocky ridge when suddenly by a stream he caught sight of a monster. Its huge face was blue and its eyes started from its head like those of a crab. They flashed with an angry gleam. Its big mouth ran from one ear to the other and looked like a dish full of blood. In it was a thick tangle of teeth two or three inches long. It was lurking by the stream, where it had just stooped to drink. The peasant could clearly hear the water slurp down its throat.

He had a terrible fright. Fortunately the monster had not yet seen him. Quickly he decided to take the roundabout way past the northern slope of the rock. This was a flat path but somewhat longer. It was taken by the villagers whenever they had wheelbarrows to push. The peasant goaded on his mule and galloped as fast as he could.

Just as he was turning the corner he suddenly heard a voice calling out behind him: 'Neighbour, wait for me!'

He turned and saw his neighbour's son. He stopped and waited.

The young neighbour said: 'Old Li is seriously ill. He

will not last much longer. His son asked me to go to the market and order a coffin. I am just on my way back.' The peasant knew that old Li had been sick for a long time and so he believed him.

The neighbour continued: 'Surely you always take the shortest route over the mountain—why are you taking this roundabout route today?'

The peasant was ill at ease: 'I wanted to go over the mountain today, but then I saw an ugly and terrifying monster, so this roundabout route is not too long.'

The neighbour said: 'Hearing you speak like that I am beginning to feel afraid myself, walking home on my own. Won't you let me sit on your mule behind you?'

The peasant consented and the neighbour mounted the mule behind him.

After a few steps he resumed: 'What did that monster look like that you saw? Tell me about it!'

The peasant said: 'I am still too upset. I will tell you everything when we've reached home.'

'If you do not want to speak,' the other replied, 'why don't you turn and look at me and tell me if I look like that monster?'

The peasant said: 'You should not make such wicked jokes! A man is not a devil.'

But the other insisted: 'Just take a look at me!'

With these words he gripped his arm hard.

The peasant turned his head and looked at him, and true enough there was the monster he had seen by the stream. In his fright he fell off the mule and remained lying on the spot unconscious.

The mule knew its way and got back home. The people in the village suspected the worst and went out along different paths to look for him. They found him at the

97

foot of the rocky slope and carried him home. It was midnight before he recovered consciousness and could tell them what had happened to him.

THERE was a scholar in Shansi who found the company of others too noisy. He therefore made his home in a Buddhist temple. But he suffered a great deal from the fact that the room was full of bedbugs, midges and fleas so that he got no sleep at nights.

Once he was resting on his bed after his meal. Then suddenly two minute horsemen appeared with plumes on their helmets. They were about two inches tall and rode horses the size of grasshoppers. On their hands they wore hawking gloves and they carried peregrines the size of flies. They galloped round the room at great speed. As the scholar was watching them another creature entered, clad like the first but carrying bow and arrows and accompanied by a hound the size of an ant. He was followed by a large throng of men on foot and on horseback, perhaps several hundreds of them. They too had hundreds of falcons and hounds with them. The midges and flies in the room flew up but they were all hunted down by the hawks. The hounds climbed on to the scholar's bed and nosed along the wall, tracking down lice and fleas and devouring them. Whatever was hiding in the crevices was spotted by them and driven out so that in a very short time nearly all the vermin was dead.

The scholar pretended to be asleep while he watched them. The falcons settled on him and the dogs scampered over his body. Presently there arrived a man in a yellow robe, with a crown like a king; he climbed up on an empty bed and installed himself there. Instantly the mounted men rode up to him, dismounted and brought him all their venison and game birds. Then they assembled in front of him in large numbers and talked to him in a strange language.

After a while the king got into a small carriage and his bodyguards hastened to saddle their horses. With a thousand cries they galloped out of the room, like beans being scattered, and a thick cloud of dust rose behind them. In an instant they were all gone but the scholar's eyes were still fixed on the spot in fright and amazement. He did not know whence they had come. He slipped on his shoes and looked all round but they had disappeared without a trace. He returned and searched about his room but there was nothing to be seen. Only on a brick by the wall was there a tiny little dog which had been left behind. Swiftly the scholar caught it. It was quite tame. He placed it in his ink box and regarded it from all sides. It had a perfectly smooth delicate skin and on its neck was a minute collar. He tried to feed it a few crumbs but it merely sniffed them and did not touch them. Then it leapt up on to the bed, and nosed out a few ticks and lice, among the seams of the clothes which it ate. Then it returned and lay down. When the night ended the scholar feared that it might have run away but there it was lying curled up as before. Whenever he laid himself to sleep the little dog would get on to his bed and kill all the vermin it could find. No fly or midge again dared to settle there. The scholar loved the little dog like a jewel.

But once he fell asleep in the daytime and the little dog had crept up to his side. When the scholar woke up he turned over, resting himself on his elbow. He felt something under him and was afraid it might be the little dog.

Hurriedly he got up and looked but the tiny dog was already dead, squashed flat like a figure cut out of paper.

But all the vermin had gone.

ONCE there was a scholar who was reading a book on the upper floor of his house. It was a cloudy, dull day and it was raining. Suddenly he noticed a small creature as brilliant as a glow-worm. It was crawling up the table. Wherever it passed it left a black singed trail, crooked like the trail of an earthworm. Slowly it crawled up on the scholar's book and the book, too, turned black. It was then that it occurred to the scholar that this could well be a dragon. He therefore carried the book to his door. There he stood watching it for a good while, but the small animal remained curled up, motionless.

Then the scholar said: 'Let no one say that I am lacking in respect.' With these words he carried the book back and placed it on his table again. He then donned formal clothes, made a deep bow and conducted it outside.

No sooner had he passed through the door than he saw the thing raise its head and suddenly straighten out. With a hissing sound it flew up from the book, describing a fiery streak. Once more it turned towards the scholar and by then its head was the size of a barrel and its body was ten feet round.

One more snaking twist and with a terrifying clap of thunder the dragon soared up into the air.

The scholar returned and tried to trace the path of the small animal. Its trail went this way and that, all the way back to his box of books.

THE gods of the Yellow River are called Tai Wang (Great Kings). For many hundred years the guardians of the river have been continually reporting the appearance of all kinds of monsters in the river's waters, sometimes in the form of cattle or horses, and whenever such a being appeared a great flood would follow. For that reason temples were built along the river. The highest-ranking of the river spirits are venerated as kings, the lower-ranking ones as generals, and hardly a day passes without some sacrifice or spectacle being performed in their honour. Whenever a dyke bursts and the breach is successfully sealed again the emperor sends his officials with offerings and ten sticks of rich Tibetan incense. This incense is burnt in a very large sacrificial cauldron in the temple courtyard and the guardians of the river and their subordinates all go into the temple to thank the gods for their help. These river gods, it is said, are the loyal and true servants of earlier rulers who lost their lives in their efforts to dam the river. After their death their spirits became river kings while their bodily shape is that of lizards, snakes and frogs.

The most powerful among these river kings is the golden dragon king. He frequently appears in the shape of a small golden snake with square head, low forehead and red patches over his eyes. He can make himself large or small at will and can cause the water to rise or fall. He will appear suddenly and disappear again just as suddenly. His home is in the estuary of the Yellow River and the Imperial

103

Canal. But in addition to him there are dozens of river kings and generals, each of whom has his definite place. All the boatmen on the Yellow River carry long lists detailing the lives and deeds of each of these river spirits. One of these river kings is called the Dammer. Two hundred years ago the Yellow River had torn a breach in the dyke and each time, just as the breach was very nearly filled again, the water burst through once more. The river guardian went up to the temple to pray. There, at night, he had a dream.

He heard a voice saying to him: 'The Dammer must come—only then will you succeed. He is a boy from among the people and he is thirteen this year.'

When the guardian awoke he was astonished at his dream.

One day he walked out again to supervise the work at the dykes. He returned in the evening.

Suddenly he heard a woman call: 'Dammer, come here!'

He immediately made enquiries and discovered that this was the name of a poor boy whom his mother had called home to dinner. He bought the boy from his parents for thirty plummet-weights of silver, and the following day Dammer was taken out to the river. He was thrown into the water and thousands of workmen immediately had to cover him with earth. In no time the breach in the dyke was sealed and the vortex calmed. Then suddenly from the middle of the river an enormous hand emerged, a good many yards long. The many workmen cried out with horror. But the river guardian and his officials fell down on their knees and prayed. Thereupon the boy was appointed a river god.

About a hundred years ago the Yellow River again burst through the dykes. As a punishment the river guardian was made to lose one button of rank and was sentenced to repair the dyke. But it seemed impossible to close the breach. The man was loyal and honest and supervised the work day and night. But each time, just as the last opening was being filled in, the dyke would collapse again and the water would burst through. The official watched it motionless, as if in a trance. His servants had to take him by the arm and lead him home. Later that evening, when the river workmen had dispersed, the guardian secretly stole out of his house and flung himself into the river. His servants hastened after him but were too late. The next day the breach was sealed. The deed was reported at Court and the official was appointed a general of the Yellow River.

The river spirits are fond of watching plays. Facing each temple there is a stage. In the hall of the temple stands the spirit tablet of the river king and on the altar in front of it is a small gilded lacquer bowl filled with clean sand. Whenever a small serpent is observed in that bowl the river king is present. The priests then strike the bell and beat the kettle-drum and read aloud from holy books. Instantly the official is notified and he at once summons a troop of actors. Before beginning their play the actors ascend to the temple, bend one knee and request the king to indicate a play. The god then chooses a play by pointing at it with his head or by writing symbols into the sand with his tail. The actors at once start to perform the play chosen.

The river god cares nothing about human happiness or sorrow. He comes suddenly and leaves suddenly, just as he pleases.

Once there was a peasant who went to market with his wheelbarrow. Suddenly the river king appeared on the peasant's straw hat without his noticing it. The people he encountered on the road called out to him and bowed before the god. Thereupon the straw hat was taken to the temple and a play was enacted.

There are a great many settlements between the outer and the inner dykes of the Yellow River. It often happens that the yellow water comes up to the edge of the inner dykes. Vertical as a wall, it advances slowly. Whenever the people see it they hasten to burn incense, bow to the water and pray, and promise a play to the river god. Then the water recedes again and the people say: 'The river god has again asked for a play.'

In that region there is a village where a rich man once lived. He built a stone wall all round the village, twenty feet high, in order to keep the water away. He did not believe in river spirits but confidently put his trust in the solid wall.

Suddenly one evening the yellow water rose and came right up to the village. The rich man ordered cannons to be fired at it. This so enraged the water that it surrounded the walls and rose until it reached the openings of the crenellations. The water roared and hissed and was about to spill over the walls. The whole village was terrified. They dragged the rich man to the wall and made him kneel down and ask forgiveness. The villagers promised a play, but this did not help; they promised to build a temple to the river god in the centre of the village and to perform plays there regularly. Only then did the water abate and gradually recede again. The crops outside the village had not suffered any damage but on the contrary, fertilized by the yellow mud, they yielded a double harvest.

Once a scholar walked across a field with a friend on his way to a relative. They happened to come past a river god's temple where a new play was just being staged. The friend suggested that they should go in and watch it. They stepped into the temple forecourt and saw two green snakes coiled round the two front columns, their heads pushed forward as though watching the spectacle. Inside the temple hall stood the altar with its bowl of sand. In it was a small snake with a golden body, a green head and red patches on its forehead. Its neck was thrust upwards and its glittering eyes were fixed steadily on the stage. The friend bowed and the scholar did likewise.

Softly he asked his friend: 'What are the names of the three river gods?'

'The one in the temple,' the other replied, 'is the golden dragon king. The two on the columns are two generals. They dare not sit in the temple at the same time as the king.'

The scholar was greatly astonished and thought to himself: 'A small serpent like that! How can it possess divine

107

strength? It would have to give me proof of its power before I revered it.'

He had scarcely conceived these secret thoughts when suddenly the small snake in the bowl raised its head above the altar. In front of the altar were two huge candles. They weighed over ten pounds each and were as thick as young trees. Their flame was as bright as that of a torch. The snake now put its head right into the candle flame which was a good inch wide and bright red. Suddenly it turned blue and divided into two tongues. That candle was so huge and its flame so hot that copper and iron would have melted in it—but it did no harm to the snake.

It then crept into the incense burner. This was an iron cauldron, so large that one could just about embrace it with both arms. Its openwork lid was adorned with a dragon ornament. The snake moved in and out through the holes of this lid and eventually threaded itself through all of them so that it gave the appearance of an embroidery in gold thread. In the end the snake had threaded itself through all the openings of the lid, large and small. To do that it must have increased its length to several dozen feet. Then it pushed out its head at the top and continued to watch the spectacle.

The scholar was afraid, bowed twice and prayed: 'Great king, you have gone to this trouble for my sake. I revere you from the bottom of my heart.'

No sooner had he uttered these words than the small snake was back in its bowl and as small as before.

In the temple at Tsining the river god's birthday was being celebrated. As a birthday present a play was being performed. The spectators stood in a solid crowd like a wall. Just then a simple peasant from the countryside came past and said in a loud voice: 'But that's only a very small worm. What foolishness to revere him as a king!'

But before he had finished speaking the snake shot out of the temple. It became bigger and bigger and wound itself three times round the stage. It grew as thick as a large bucket and its head was like that of a dragon. Its eyes glittered like golden lamps and its tongue spewed out red flames. It stretched and contracted, making the stage seem as if it was about to collapse. The actors interrupted their music and fell down on their knees in prayer. The whole crowd was seized with terror and bowed deep to the ground. Then a few old men came and threw the peasant to the ground and whipped him and kicked him until he was half dead. At last he threw himself down before the snake and prayed to it. There was a noise as when a firework is let off. It went on for some time and then the snake was gone.

East of Shantung lies the city of Tengchow. It has a viewing tower with a great temple. Below it lies the water city with its water gate in the north through which the high tide enters the city. By this gate a troop of coastguards is stationed.

Once there was an officer who had been posted there as captain. He used to serve with the army and had not been long at his new post. He was giving a dinner party for a few friends. Outside the pavilion was a large stone the shape of a table. Suddenly there appeared on it a small wriggling snake; it was spotted green and had red patches on its square head. The soldiers wanted to kill the beast and the captain strode out to see what was happening.

Then he laughed: 'Do not harm him! That is the river god of Tsining. When I was stationed there he would visit me occasionally and I always performed sacrifices and plays in his honour. Now he has come here specially to wish me luck and visit his old friend.'

There was a band in the camp and its men used to sing and dance every bit as well as a real troupe of actors. The captain hurriedly made them enact a spectacle while he prepared another festive meal with wine and choice dishes and invited the river god to make himself at home.

Night was falling and the river god still did not seem anxious to leave.

The captain thereupon stepped up to him, bowed and said: 'We are a long way here from the Yellow River and these people have never yet heard your name. I am greatly honoured by your visit. But these women and fools who are crowding round, gaping, are afraid to hear about you. Well, you have visited your old friend and can now return again.'

With these words he commanded a litter to be brought; the kettle-drums were beaten and incense was burned, and finally nine guns were fired as a festive send-off. The little snake eventually stepped into the litter and the captain followed. Thus they came to the harbour and while the farewells were being said the snake was already streaking through the water. It had become much larger than before and, nodding its head to the captain, it disappeared.

Then there were doubts and questions: 'Surely the river god lives a thousand miles away—how did he get here?'

But the captain replied: 'He is so powerful that he can get anywhere, and besides there is a waterway leading from his home to the sea. To come down that waterway and swim across the sea is a matter of a moment to him.'

TWENTY miles east of Tsingchao is the Maiden Lake. It covers a few square miles. It is surrounded by thick clumps of green shrubs and by tall forests. Its water is clear and deep blue. Often all kinds of strange beasts are seen in it. The people of the region have built a temple there for the dragon princess and in times of drought they make a pilgrimage there to pray.

West of Tsingchao, 200 miles away, is another lake whose god is called Chao Na and can work many miracles. In the Tang period there was an official in Tsingchao by name of Chou Pao. During his term of office it happened that, in the fifth month, the clouds suddenly rose, piled up one upon another like mountains, with dragons and serpents winding between them. The clouds drifted to and fro between the two lakes. There was a storm and a downpour with thunder and lightning so that houses collapsed and trees were uprooted. Some people were killed and great damage was done to the crops. Chou Pao accepted responsibility and prayed to heaven for the people to be forgiven.

On the fifth day of the sixth month he was sitting in his council chamber, dispensing justice. Suddenly he felt tired and sleepy. He took off his hat and lay down on the cushions. No sooner had he closed his eyes than he saw a warrior standing on the steps outside the hall, wearing helmet and armour and carrying a halberd. The warrior reported: 'There is a lady outside who desires to enter.' Chou Pao asked him: 'And who are you?' The man replied: 'I am your door-keeper. I have held this office in the invisible world for many years.' Just then two men in green came running up the steps, knelt before him and said: 'Our mistress has arrived to visit you.' Chou Pao rose to his feet. He saw before him delightful clouds from which a gentle rain trickled down, and an unfamiliar perfume captivated him. Then he saw a woman in a simple robe but of extraordinary beauty floating down from on high, with a retinue of many serving women. They were all clean and neat and were in attendance on the lady as if she were a princess. As she entered the hall she raised her arm in salute. Chou Pao went forward to meet her and invited her to sit down. From all sides coloured clouds floated in and a purple mist filled the courtyard. Chou Pao ordered wine and food to be served and entertained his guest most munificently. But the goddess sat there with furrowed brow, staring fixedly in front of her, and looking exceedingly sad. Then she rose to her feet, went close to him and said with a blush: 'I have lived near here for many years. The injustice I have suffered induces me to overstep the bounds of propriety and lends me courage to put my request to you. Yet I know not whether you want to save me.'

'May I hear what the trouble is?' asked Chou Pao. 'If I can help at all I shall be pleased to be at your disposal.'

The goddess said: 'My family has been living in the depths of the eastern sea for centuries. Then, to our misfortune, our riches aroused the envy of humans. So Pi-lo's ancestor almost totally exterminated our tribe by fire. Our ancestors had to flee and go into hiding, and there could be no question of vengeance. A short while ago our enemy So Pi-lo himself tried to present an imperial letter at the cave of the Tungting Lake. On the pretext of

113

desiring pearls and treasure he tried to penetrate into the dragon castle and wipe out our tribe. Fortunately a sage discovered his treacherous intent and prevented him from entering. Then Lo Tsi-chun and his brothers were sent out in his place. Our family feared that they might come to harm in the future and therefore moved to the far west. My father did a great deal for the human race and he is deeply revered among them. I am his ninth daughter. At the age of sixteen I was married to the youngest son of the rock dragon. My good husband had a hot temper and therefore frequently offended against good manners, and before I had lived a year with him heaven's punishment fell upon him. I was left alone and returned to my parents' house. My father wanted to marry me off a second time, but I wished to remain faithful to my husband and swore not to obey my father. My parents were angry and I had to leave home to escape their wrath. That was three years ago. Who would have thought that the common dragon Chao Na, who is seeking a wife for his youngest brother, would force a marriage gift upon me? I refused to accept it, but Chao Na succeeded in gaining my father's favour and was determined to have his way. My father, caring nothing for my wishes, promised me to him. Then the dragon Chao Na and his youngest brother came to carry me off by force of arms. I opposed him with my fifty faithful followers and we battled in the fields outside the city. We were defeated and I fear that the rascal will now shame me so that I can never face my late husband again. That is why I plucked up my courage to implore you to lend me your soldiers so I can repel my enemies and preserve my widowhood. If you will help me I shall be grateful to you to the end of my days.'

114

Chou Pao replied: 'You are of noble family—surely you must have relations who would hasten to your aid in your hour of need. Why do you have to turn to a mortal human?'

'My tribe is indeed famous and numerous. If I sent word to them and they came to my help then indeed they would crush that worm Chao Na just as one crushes garlic. But my late husband offended the heavens and he has not yet been pardoned. Moreover, I have opposed my parents' wishes so that I cannot appeal to my own family for help. You will understand my desperate straits.' Thereupon Chou Pao promised her his help and the princess thanked him and departed.

When he awoke he sighed for a long time at the thought of his strange experience. The following day he dispatched fifteen hundred soldiers to keep watch along the Maiden Lake.

On the seventh day of the sixth month Chou Pao rose early. It was still dark outside and it seemed to him that he saw a man standing outside the curtain. He asked him who he was. The man replied: 'I am the Princess's adviser. Yesterday you were good enough to send us soldiers to save us in our adversity. But these were all living humans. They cannot do battle with the invisible. You must send us dead soldiers—only then shall we prevail.'

Chou Pao reflected for a while and agreed: 'Of course it must be so.' He ordered his army scribe to scan the lists for those of his soldiers who had been killed in battle. These numbered two thousand foot troops and five hundred horsemen. He appointed a dead officer, Mëng Yüan, to be their commander, wrote his order on a piece of paper which he burnt, and in this manner made the troops available to the princess. He then recalled the living

115

soldiers. As he was inspecting them in his courtyard on their return one man suddenly collapsed unconscious. Not until the following morning did he recover. When he was questioned he reported: 'I saw a man in red robes advance towards me and address me as follows: "Our princess is grateful for your master's kind help. Yet she has one more request—that is why I am instructed to call on you." I followed him to the temple. The princess bade me advance and said to me: "I am sincerely grateful to your master for sending me his ghost soldiers. Only their commander Mëng Yüan is not efficient. Yesterday the raiders came with three thousand men and Mëng Yüan was defeated by them. When you return and see your master tell him please that I request him to send me a good commander. Then perhaps my troubles will be over." Thereupon I was conducted back and recovered consciousness.'

When Chou Pao heard these words, which strangely tallied with his dream, he decided to make a test. He therefore chose his victorious general Chong Fu to succeed Mëng Yüan. In the evening he burnt incense, poured a libation of wine and surrendered the general's soul to the princess.

On the 26th of the month news came from the general's camp that he had suddenly died at midnight on the 13th. Chou Pao was afraid and sent a man to look at the body. The man reported that the dead general's heart was not yet cold. Moreover, in spite of the hot summer weather, the body was showing no traces of decomposition. Chou Pao therefore commanded that he should not be buried.

One night an icy ghostly wind sprang up which whirled up the sand and stones, snapped trees and blew down houses. The crops in the fields were all flattened. It went on all day long. In the end there was a loud crash of

116

thunder, the sky cleared again and the clouds dispersed. At about the same time the dead general began to breath again on his bed, with a rattle in his throat, and when his family came to look at him he had come to life again.

They asked him what had happened and he told them: 'First I saw a man in purple robe on a black horse arriving with a great retinue. He dismounted at my door. In his hand he held a letter of appointment which he presented to me with these words: "Our princess requests you respectfully to become her general. I trust you will not refuse." Then he produced gifts and piled them up on the steps—jasper, brocade and silken clothes, saddles, horses, helmets and armour. I wanted to decline but he would not accept a refusal and urged me to get into a carriage. We drove for a hundred miles when a troop of three hundred armoured horsemen caught up with us. They escorted us to a great city. Outside the city a tent had been set up with a band playing in it. A high official served me a cup of wine as a welcome. When I entered the city there was a solid wall of onlookers. Servants ran to and fro carrying orders. We must have passed through a dozen gates before we reached the castle. There I was asked to get out and change my clothes in order to meet the princess. The princess wanted to receive me as her guest. I considered this too much honour and saluted her from the bottom of the stairs. But she invited me to sit down with her in the hall. She sat upright, in incomparable beauty, surrounded by servant women with painted faces and rich jewellery. They were plucking strings and playing flutes. A host of servants were standing around, with golden belts and purple tassels, awaiting orders. Vast throngs were standing outside the palace. Five or six ladies were sitting in a circle around the princess as I was

117

conducted to my place by a general. The princess addressed me as follows: "I have asked you here to entrust you with the command of my army. If you break my enemy's strength I shall richly reward you." I pledged my obedience. Thereupon wine was brought in and the meal served to the strains of music. While we were at table a messenger arrived. "The robber Chao Na has invaded our country with ten thousand men on foot and on horseback. He is approaching our city by various roads. His advance is marked by smoke and columns of fire." The guests all went pale with fright when they heard the news. And the princess said: "That is the enemy who made me turn to you. Save me from my distress!" She then gave me two warhorses, a golden suit of armour and the insignia of a general and bowed to me. I left her gratefully, summoned the commanders, ordered the army to line up and moved out of the city. At a few keypoints I placed my troops in an ambush. Already the enemy was approaching in great strength, carefree and unconcerned, intoxicated with his earlier victories. I first sent forward the least good of my soldiers, who allowed themselves to be beaten in order to draw the enemy on. He was next engaged by lightly-armed men who fell back skirmishing. In this way he was caught in the ambush. Gongs and drums sounded at the same time and from all sides the ring closed round him. The army of the invaders suffered a great defeat. Their dead littered the ground like hemp stalks, but the small Chao Na succeeded in slipping through. I ordered my light cavalry to pursue him and he was captured in front of his generals' tents. I hastened to send a report to the princess. I reviewed the prisoners outside her palace. All the people, noble and humble, came to congratulate her. Chao Na was to be executed in the market-place. But suddenly a mounted messenger arrived with an order from the princess's father that Chao Na should be pardoned. The princess dared not refuse obedience. So he was sent back to his own country, having first been made to forswear all evil intentions. I was showered with favours for my victory and given an estate with three thousand peasants. I received a palace, carriages and horses, all kinds of jewels, men and women servants, gardens and forests, flags and suits of armour. And the unit commanders were all rewarded according to merit. The following day a banquet was given which was attended also by the noble ladies staying with the princess. Drinking went on until late at night. The princess with her own hand filled her precious cup, ordered a maid-servant to carry it over to me, and said to me: "Widowed at an early age, I opposed the will of my strict father and fled from him to this place. Here I was hard pressed by that rascal Chao Na and was about to suffer humiliation and shame at his hands. But for your master's great kind-ness and your own bravery I should have shared the fate of that princess who, married against her will, remained silent to the end of her life." She then began to thank me and tears of emotion rolled down her cheeks. I bowed to her and requested some leave to look after my family. I was granted a month. The following day I was dismissed with a great entourage. A pavilion had been set up out-side the city where I was offered a parting drink. Thus I rode away, and as I reached our gate there was a thunder clap and I awoke.'

The general thereupon wrote a report to Chou Pao, con-veying to him the princess's thanks. From then onwards he no longer concerned himself with the affairs of the world but set his house in order and made it over to his wife and his son. When the month was up he died without having been ill.

On that day one of his officers was travelling on the road. Suddenly he saw a thick cloud of dust swirling up and flags and banners darkening the sun. A thousand horsemen were escorting a man who sat in his saddle proudly and heroically. When he saw his face he recognized the general Chong Fu. Hurriedly he stepped to the edge of the road to make way for the procession. They galloped towards the Maiden Lake, where they vanished.

In the Tang period there lived a man by name of Liu Yi who had failed his doctor's examination. So he set out on his homeward journey. He had covered about six or seven miles when a bird flew up in a field. His horse shied and bolted some ten miles before it would halt again. When it stopped Liu Yi saw a woman tending sheep on a mountainside. He looked at her: she was exceedingly beautiful but her features betrayed secret grief. Curious, he asked her the reason for her sorrow.

The woman began to sob and said: 'Fortune has turned its back on me; I have fallen into adversity and disgrace. But since you have shown the kindness of asking me I will tell you everything openly. I am the youngest daughter of the dragon ruler of the Tungting Lake and was married to the second son of the dragon king of the Ching river. But my husband was frivolously inclined and had an intrigue with a maidservant. He then cast me out. I complained to my parents-in-law, but they were so blinded by their love for their son that they did nothing. When I entreated them more urgently they both got angry and I was sent here to tend the sheep.' When she had finished speaking she burst out sobbing bitterly and quite uncontrollably. Then she continued: 'The Tungting Lake is a long way from here, but I have found out that you pass it on your homeward journey. I would like you to give a letter to my father, but I am not sure whether you will do this for me?'

Liu Yi replied: 'Your words have most deeply stirred

my heart. I wish I had wings to fly away with you. I will gladly deliver your letter to your father. But the Tungting Lake is vast and wide—how shall I be able to find him?'

'On the southern shore of the lake stands an orange tree,' the woman replied. 'The people call it the tree of sacrifice. When you get there you must take off your belt and swing it three times at the orange tree; then someone will appear whom you may follow. If you see my father please tell him in what misery you have found me and that I crave his help.'

Then she produced a letter from her bosom and gave it to Liu Yi. She bowed to him and with a deep sigh looked towards the east. Liu Yi, too, found the tears running down his cheeks. He took the letter and put it in his satchel.

Then he asked: 'I do not understand why you must tend sheep. Surely the gods do not slaughter animals?'

'These are no ordinary sheep,' said the woman: they are rain servants.'

'What are rain servants?'

'They are thunder rams,' the woman said.

And when he looked more closely he saw that the animals strode about proudly and wildly, quite unlike ordinary sheep.

Liu Yi added: 'When I have taken this letter to your father so at some future date you are able to return safely to the Tungting Lake, you must not then treat me like a stranger.'

The woman replied: 'How could I ever treat you as a stranger? You shall be my dearest friend!'

With these words they parted.

After a month Liu Yi reached the Tungting Lake and

122

asked his way to the orange tree. When he had found it he took off his belt and struck it three times against the tree. At once a warrior emerged from the lake's waves.

He asked: 'Where do you come from, honoured guest?'

Liu Yi replied: 'I have an important message and want to see the king.'

The warrior motioned towards the water and it instantly turned into a solid road for Liu Yi to ride along. In front of them appeared the dragon castle with its thousand gates. Strange flowers and rare grasses grew in profusion everywhere. The warrior bade him wait at the entrance to a great hall.

He asked: 'What is the name of this place?'

'This is the hall of spirits,' was the reply. Liu Yi looked about him. All the precious things of the human world were present here in lavish magnificence. The columns were of white quartz inlaid with green jasper; the seats were of coral, the curtains were of translucent rock crystal, and the windows of polished glass adorned with rich scroll-work. The vaulting of the ceiling was decorated with amber. A strange perfume hung in the air and the whole room was steeped in a mysterious twilight.

Liu Yi was kept waiting a long time to see the king. In reply to his questions the warrior said: 'My lord is pleased to discuss the sacred book of the fire with the sun priest on top of the coral tower at this moment. No doubt he will soon be finished.'

Liu Yi went on asking: 'Why the sacred book of the fire?'

The reply was: 'Our lord is a dragon. The dragons are mighty by the power of water. With a single wave they can cover mountains and valleys. The priest is a human. Humans are mighty by the power of fire. With a single

123

torch they can burn down the greatest palaces. Fire and water are at war because in their nature they are opposed. That is why our lord converses with the priest, in order to find a way in which fire and water may supplement each other.'

Before they had finished a man appeared in a purple robe with a sceptre of jasper in his hand.

The warrior said: 'This is my lord.'

Liu Yi bowed before him.

The king said: 'Surely you are a living human? What brings you here?'

Liu Yi gave his name and related: 'I was in the capital and there failed my examination. As I passed the Ching river I saw your beloved daughter tending sheep in the wilderness. The wind had tousled her hair and the rain had drenched it. I could not bear to see her misery and therefore addressed her. She complained to me that her husband had cast her out and she cried bitterly. Then she gave me a letter. That, sire, is why I have come to see you.'

With these words he produced the letter and handed it to the king. When the king had read it he hid his face in his sleeve and said with a sigh: 'This is my fault. I chose a bad husband for her. I was anxious to get my daughter married as soon as possible and now I have thrust her into shame and humiliation in a distant land. You are a stranger, yet you were ready to help her in her need; for that I am sincerely grateful to you.' Then he began to sob again and all those around him shed tears. The king now handed the letter to a servant who took it into the interior of the palace. After a short while loud laments were heard from the inner rooms.

The king was startled and turned to one of his officials:

124

'Go and tell them in there not to cry so noisily; I am afraid Chientang might hear them.'

'And who is Chientang?' asked Liu Yi.

'He is my beloved brother,' said the king. 'He used to be the ruler of the Chientang river, but now he has been deposed.'

Liu Yi asked: 'Why should he not hear about this business?'

'He is so wild and impetuous,' was the reply, 'that I am afraid he might do great damage. The great flood which covered the earth for nine years during the reign of the Emperor Yao was caused by him in his anger. Because he had a quarrel with a heavenly ruler he caused a great flood which reached to the summits of the five tall mountains. Then the lord was angry with him and gave him into my charge. I had to chain him to a column of the palace.'

Before he could finish a sudden uproar broke out, a noise rending the sky and shaking the earth and causing the whole palace to tremble, and causing smoke and clouds to billow out with a fierce hissing. A red dragon burst in, a thousand feet long, with flashing eyes, a blood-red tongue, scarlet scales and a fiery beard. The column to which he had been fettered was dragged along by him on a chain through the air. Snow, rain and hail were swirling in wild confusion. There was a thunderclap and the dragon soared up towards the sky and disappeared.

Liu Yi fell to the ground with fright. The king helped him up with his own hands and said: 'No need to be afraid! That is my brother hurrying off to the Ching river in anger. We shall soon have good news.'

He thereupon commanded wine and food to be brought in and to be served to the guest. When the cup had gone

125

the rounds three times a gentle breeze sprang up with a whisper and fine rain fell softly. A young man in a purple robe and tall hat entered. At his side he wore a sword. He had a manly and heroic bearing. Behind him walked a girl of striking beauty in a misty-fragrant garment. When Liu Yi looked at her he recognized her as the dragon princess he had met on his journey. A crowd of girls dressed in red received her, with much laughing and giggling and led her off into the interior of the palace. The ruler meanwhile introduced the young man, saying: 'This is Chientang, my brother.'

Chientang thanked him for conveying the message. He then turned to his brother and said: 'I fought those damned dragons and utterly defeated them.'

'How many did you kill?'

'Six hundred thousand.'

'Was farmland damaged?'

'Over some eight hundred miles.'

'And where is the heartless husband?'

'I have eaten him.'

Then the king was horrified and said: 'What that vile knave did was, of course, intolerable. But you have been rather too rough on him. You must not do such a thing again in future.' Chientang gave him his promise.

That night a great feast was held at the castle for Liu Yi. The banquet was heightened by music and dancing. A thousand warriors with banners and spears in their hands stepped forward. Trombones and trumpets were sounded, gongs and kettle-drums were beaten, and a war dance was performed. The music expressed how Chientang had broken through the enemy ranks. At the mere sound of it the guest's hair stood on end in fright. Then, by contrast, came the soft sound of strings, flutes and golden bells.

Clad in red and green silk, a thousand girls performed a dance, symbolizing the princess's return. The notes were like a song, like sobbing, like laments, like grief, and all those who heard them were reduced to tears. The king of the Tungting Lake was highly pleased. Then he raised his cup and drank the guest's health until the wine had washed away all their worries. The two rulers thanked their guest in verse and Liu Yi for his part replied in a rhymed toast. The crowds of courtiers in the palace applauded. Then the king of the Tungting Lake brought out a blue cloud box in which the water-cleaving rhinoceros horn lay. Chientang brought out a slab of red amber with a carbuncle on it. This he presented to the guest, and everyone else in the palace likewise heaped up presents by his side—embroideries, brocades and pearls. Surrounded by gleam and glitter Liu Yi sat there, thanking everybody with a smile. When the meal was over he slept in the castle of frozen splendour.

The following day another banquet was given. Chientang, a little drunk, was lolling back in his seat and said: 'The daughter of the king of the Tungting Lake is trim and pretty. She was unfortunate enough to be cast out by her husband. Today her marriage is dissolved. I should like to find her another husband. If you agreed to be her husband this might be of advantage to you. If you are not so inclined you are free to go your way and if ever we meet again we shall not know each other.'

Liu Yi was annoyed at the offhand manner in which Chientang spoke to him. The blood rose to his head and he retorted: 'I acted as messenger because I took pity on the princess and not in order to gain a personal advantage. To kill a husband and abduct his wife—that is something an honest man does not do. Even though I am no more than an ordinary human I would rather die than act on your words.'

Chientang got to his feet, apologized and said: 'I spoke too hastily. I hope you will forgive me.' And the lord of the Tungting Lake likewise spoke to him kindly and rebuked Chientang for his rude speech. The subject of the marriage was not touched upon again.

The following day Liu Yi took his leave and the queen of the Tungting Lake gave another banquet in honour of his departure.

With tears in her eyes the queen said to Liu Yi: 'My daughter owes you a great debt of gratitude and we have had no chance of repaying you. Now you are leaving us and we are letting you go with a heavy heart.'

Thereupon she ordered the princess to thank Liu Yi.

The princess rose, blushing, bowed to Liu Yi and said: 'We shall probably never meet again.' Then the tears choked her.

Liu Yi had resisted her uncle's impetuous urgings but as he now saw the princess standing in all her loveliness he regretted it in his heart. However, he controlled himself and departed. The treasure which he took with him was immense. The king himself and his brother escorted him as far as the river.

Back home, even though he sold only one-hundredth part of what he had received, his fortune amounted to millions and he became richer than any of his neighbours. He was twice married, but both his wives died after a short while. So he lived on in the capital, alone. He was looking for a new wife. A marriage broker came to see him and told him that in the north there was a widow living with her daughter. The father had embraced Taoism in his old age and had disappeared in the clouds and

128

never returned. The mother was now living with her daughter in reduced circumstances, but because the girl was beautiful beyond all measure she was looking for a noble son-in-law.

Liu Yi agreed and the marriage was arranged. When, on the evening of his wedding, he saw his bride unveiled she looked exactly like the dragon princess. He asked her, but she only smiled and said nothing.

After a year she gave birth to a son. Then she said to her husband: 'Today I will confess to you—I am really the princess of the Tungting Lake. After you had spurned my uncle's offer and parted from us, I became ill with longing and was near death. My parents wanted to send word to you, but they were afraid you might object to my origin. Thus I was married to you disguised as a human girl. Until now I did not dare confess this to you. But now that I have borne you a son I hope that you will transfer your love for him to his mother.'

It seemed to Liu Yi that he was suddenly awakening from a deep stupor. And the two loved each other deeply.

One day the wife said: 'If you want to live with me eternally we cannot remain in the human world. We dragons reach an age of ten thousand years and you shall share our long life. Come back with me to the Tungting Lake!'

Ten years passed and no one knew where Liu Yi had vanished to. One day, when a relation of his was sailing over the Tungting Lake, a blue mountain suddenly emerged from the surface of the waters.

The sailors called out in alarm: 'There is no mountain at this spot; it must be a water demon!'

While they were arguing and keeping a look-out the mountain came closer to the ship and from its summit a brightly coloured boat glided down into the water. Along the two sides stood fairies and in the middle sat a man. It was Liu Yi. He waved his hand to his cousin and the cousin gathered up his robes and stepped across into his boat. But at that moment it suddenly changed back into a mountain and on that mountain was a magnificent castle and there, standing in the castle was Liu Yi, surrounded by music and brilliant colours.

They greeted each other and Liu Yi said to his cousin: 'It is only a moment since we last met and your hair is grey already.'

The cousin replied: 'You are a blessed god, but I have a corruptible body. That is fate.'

But Liu Yi gave him fifty pills and said: 'Each pill will prolong your life by a year. When these years have expired dwell no longer in the world of earthly dust which knows nothing but misery and suffering, but come and join me.'

He then sailed with him across the lake and vanished.

His cousin withdrew from the world and after fifty years, when he had swallowed all the pills, he too disappeared and was never seen again.

To the west of Kiauchou Bay there is a mountain village which is called Fox Hole. East of the village is a high rock and through that rock runs a cave as round as the full moon. The cave runs through the whole mountain like a tunnel, about half a mile long, and emerges on the far side. The old folk believe that a lot of foxes and weasels live in that cave. For that reason no one dare enter it and the village owes its name to the cave.

One day two peasants from the district were walking to the city.

As they passed Fox Hole they pointed towards the entrance to the cave and one of them said in jest: 'If someone lit a good fire here the foxes and weasels would all be burnt to death.'

The other, who was a farmer, burst into noisy laughter and said: 'With the fire burning in front and the smoke coming out at the back, that would be real fun!'

As they were returning from the city the farmer suddenly burst into bitter tears. He referred to himself by his own name and a voice not his own issued from his lips: 'I am your father. I lost my life in pitiful circumstances. Today is my chance to visit my home again.' Then the voice called for the farmer's mother, and when she came he took her by her hand and wept bitterly and talked to her about things that had happened earlier in his life. Then he said: 'I am hungry. Have some wine and food served to me quickly! But it must be a chicken.'

The farmer's mother really believed that this was the

spirit of her husband because it spoke to her of things which no one else knew. So she too started to weep with emotion. But the farmer's wife did not like the look of things and, as he insisted on having a chicken for his meal, she suspected that her husband might be possessed by a fox.

She therefore told him curtly: 'We have no wine in the house and the chickens are broody. I will cook you some gruel. After all, my dear father-in-law, you are a blessed spirit and it is your duty therefore to help us instead of running us into unnecessary expense.'

At this, angry words came from her husband's lips: 'That woman has no respect. That stuff you have fermenting in that large barrel—surely that is wine? And you have a whole coop full of chickens. You feed them a bucket of grain every day. Why will you not sacrifice a single one to please your deceased father?'

The mother could bear it no longer. She ordered her daughter-in-law to bring a chicken and wine and the possessed one began to eat and drink. But as he was eating his pointed lips twitched like those of a weasel and all those who saw it laughed surreptitiously. There was a lad in the neighbourhood who was tall and strong. He now picked up a knife and called out: 'Are you not the old weasel? Are you not just pretending to be the deceased father? If you don't speak the truth at once I will kill you.'

When he heard these words the farmer's face was distorted with fear and alarm: 'It is true I am not his old father,' he said, 'but this man walked past our cave with a peasant today and said some wicked things, such as wanting to smoke out our whole tribe. That is why I have come to pay him back. And one of us has come with me

132

and he now possesses the peasant. But since you have treated me to a meal I will now leave and collect my friend as well.'

With these words the farmer dropped on his bed and only slowly regained consciousness.

Much the same had happened at the peasant's house. As he was about to lie down after supper his eyes suddenly went rigid and his mind was confused. He was thrown to the ground, then he jumped up again and leapt up several feet in the air so that he struck his head on the beams. He then beat his breast and began to berate himself: 'We have lived in this mountain cave since time immemorial, and you want to smoke us out!' his voice said. Then he leapt in the air again and no one could hold him. His parents began to say prayers and ordered incense to be burnt and wine to be brought for sacrifice. But there was no change until the peasant lad walked in with his knife.

He spoke to him and said: 'Those two were only joking. They never intended to smoke you out really. Now you have paid them back quite enough. Your friend is waiting for you outside. Now hop it, or you shall have a taste of my knife!'

Then a timid voice came from the peasant's throat: 'I am just leaving, I am just leaving.'

From that time onwards the two were never troubled again.

ONCE there was a peasant who was young and strong. Late one evening he was returning from the market. His path took him past a rich man's estate in which there were many tall buildings. Suddenly he saw something bright floating into the air and glowing like a crystal pearl. He wondered what it was and climbed over the wall into the garden. There was no one to be seen. Only in the distance was there something rather like a dog gazing up at the moon. Whenever it exhaled its breath a fiery ball came out of its mouth and rose up to the moon. When it drew in its breath again the ball floated down until the beast caught it in its mouth again. Thus it went on ceaselessly. Just then the peasant realized that the beast was a fox who was producing the elixir of life. He hid in the grass and waited for the fiery ball to come down again to roughly the height of his head. Then he swiftly stepped out and snatched it away. He swallowed it at once. He could feel the heat descending through his chest all the way to his stomach. When the fox saw what had happened he was angry, and glared at the peasant, but he feared his strength. He dared not attack him but went off furiously.

From that day onwards the young peasant was able to make himself invisible, to see ghosts and devils and to have contact with the other world. When people were sick and had lost consciousness he could call back their souls and when someone had committed a sin he could plead for him. In this way he made a great deal of money.

134

When he had reached his fiftieth year he withdrew from all these things and no longer practised his skills. One summer evening he was sitting in his courtyard enjoying the fresh cool air. He drank one cup of wine after another all by himself. By midnight he was totally drunk. He rested his palms on the ground and vomited. Suddenly he felt as if someone had slapped his back. He vomited more violently and finally the ball of fire jerked out of his throat.

The fox picked it up and said: 'For thirty years you enjoyed my treasure. From a poor peasant lad you have become a rich man. Now you have all you need. I want my treasure back.'

At this the man was completely sober. But the fox had gone.

IT is said that when a fox makes the elixir of life he can change his shape. But he must escape death by thunder three times before he can achieve it, and that is not easy. However, there are several ways in which a fox can escape his fate. Sometimes he may hide in the house of a nobleman or under the bed of a scholar or monk.

Anyone who saves his life in such peril is richly rewarded and his whole family benefits from it. If anyone kills him without good reason then he will be pursued by his everlasting hatred and the fox will not rest until that man and his whole family are ruined. Thus the foxes clearly show their likes and dislikes. Some of them are even superior to humans in that they know that they are up against an inexorable fate for which no one can be held responsible.

There was once a huntsman who was resting in a cool melon field on a hot summer's day. Suddenly black clouds appeared on all sides. Thunder and lightning succeeded each other continuously. A fiery ball rose from the earth, leaving behind a smell of sulphur. It rose to the top of a tree and then fell down again. When the huntsman looked more closely he saw a huge fox in the branches of the tree; in his front paws he held a small red flag. Whenever a fiery thunderbolt came too close to him he brushed the little flag over it and the fire instantly sank to the ground. This went on for a good hour and the thunder was unable to hurt the fox.

The huntsman's gaze was still fixed on that strange

spectacle when a black cloud descended to the ground. Curled up in it was a dragon. It was hovering just above his head. Then the dragon turned towards the tree. Then it turned about again and approached the huntsman.

The huntsman was frightened at first but then he thought to himself: 'He is probably asking my help.' So he loaded his shotgun and took aim. The dragon once more made for the top of the tree and the flash of lightning went with him. But the fox again parried it with his little flag. Quickly the huntsman fired his gun and hit the fox. The little red flag fell to the ground. At once there was a violent clap of thunder and the fox was consumed by the fire.

The huntsman picked up the little flag and looked at it. It was made from an old woman's skirt. Evidently the dragon had kept away from it because it was unclean.

ONCE there was a man who greatly venerated foxes. He had built an altar for them in his room and there he burnt incense every day. Every day of the year he placed on it food and drink offerings of chickens and wine. As a result his possessions increased from day to day. In his trading he always made a big profit and whenever he planted a crop it yielded a double harvest.

At the time of the Taiping rebellion the man took his entire store of grain to the city, to the house of a kinsman, to escape looting. His kinsman, however, had a son who was a drunkard and a gambler. He stole the man's grain, sold it, and got through the money in no time. Altogether he must have helped himself to a hundred bushels. When the bandits had left the neighbourhood the man took his grain back home. One might have thought that, upon measuring it, he would have noticed that it had diminished. But it had not only not diminished but in fact increased by nearly a hundred bushels. From then onwards the man grew so rich that throughout the region he was known as the rich man by the grace of the foxes.

Now this man had a neighbour who had always been wealthy. He was a strong brave man and skilled in the art of swordsmanship. He could lift six men into the air at a time and carry them away. He was fond of wine and company, and whenever warriors came to the neighbourhood they would visit him. His house was always full of guests, so that, over the years, his fortune diminished a little after all. In the end he grew old and his strength declined. Then a fox began to plague his home. But this fox did not manifest himself by possessing a human but simply caused all kinds of trouble. He would not leave the occupants of the house alone. One moment he would appear outside a window as a devil's mask, the next a blue hand would appear through the door and snatch away food, or else a millstone would leap up and spin to the ground with a loud crash, or else dog and chicken dirt would appear in the food just as it was being cooked. One moment lumps of clay the size of a hand would crash down from the ceiling while the women were working in the house, the next a glow would appear under the eaves and when it was challenged bright flames would burst from it. One day when the housewife complained angrily about these happenings tongues of flame leaped out from under her skirts. The occupants of the house were for ever falling ill with fright.

The spirits affected all the members of the family except the master of the house whom, evidently, the fox dared not molest. But even he was powerless against him.

There was a magician in the next village who was reputed to be able to drive out the foxes. He was summoned. But before he would come he demanded ten plummet-weights of silver.

Only then did he start on his magic in the hall. He painted runes and recited magic formulas and then at last the fox's bark was heard.

The magician reached out his hand for him but then he said with surprise: 'He got away. I merely pulled out a handful of his hairs.'

And true enough in his hand was a fistful of hair.

No sooner had the magician left the house than the

spook started anew. It seems probable that he himself produced the barking of the fox and had the fox's hair hidden up his sleeve all the time.

But the master of the house had made up his mind to get hold of the fox at all costs. He therefore armed his sons and servants with shotguns. Whenever a spirit appeared they fired at it. So long as the firing continued the spirit did nothing, but the moment the firing ceased it started again. In short, they made no headway against it.

One of the tenant farmers of the family had a wife who was a witch. One day she said: 'The fox god likes humans to revere him. You should not fight against him. You should serve him a meal as an offering, and then I shall entreat the fox god to make peace with you and to turn all your sufferings to joy.'

The master of the household would have no truck with her, but his wife secretly agreed with the witch. One of the rooms was prepared, choice wine and exquisite dishes were placed there, and the witch spent the night in the room on her own. When the next day dawned and the others entered the room they found the food and wine gone and the witch completely drunk.

Slurring her words she said: 'Quite a number of great gods came and sat down and partook of the wine and the food and enjoyed themselves. They even allowed me to eat with them. I told them about the good intentions of the master of the house and advised them to make peace with him. This the gods promised to do.'

But before she had even finished speaking a stone came flying in from outside and landed on the table, smashing all plates and cups. The witch covered her face with her hands and rushed out.

During the night one of the servants had been eaves-dropping on her. She had not said any prayers at all but had secretly invited her son and together with him had eaten and drunk her fill, and anything that was left over her son had carried off in a basket.

Eventually a young maid servant was possessed by the fox and was compelled to steal food and jewellery. For that she was beaten by her mistress. Then the urge came upon her to hang herself in the mill. Several times she was saved, but in the end she hanged herself. The maid-servant's father started a law suit. As a result the entire fortune of the family was lost and the master of the house was reduced to penury.

He had to sell his house and move into a simple thatched hut.

One evening he was sitting in his courtyard on his own, enjoying a cup of wine. Suddenly he saw something black cowering on the wall, about the size of a dog, with eyes glinting like lightning. The master acted as though he had not seen it but secretly reached for his horsewhip. Then he struck at it with all his might and hit it right across the forehead. It turned a somersault and fell to the ground on the far side of the wall. When a search was made it had disappeared. That was the end of the spirit. The family, however, had been reduced to poverty.

GREAT Father Hu is a spirit fox. When the foxes have almost finished making the elixir of life they can work miracles. They are then entered in the imperial list of sacrifices.

When the Manchu first came to China they made Mukden their ancestral seat and there established a big temple which was entrusted to a high dignitary. Everything there is just as in the imperial temple in Peking. In this temple stand tripods and sacrificial vessels, all of them wrought of gold, silver and precious stones and worth many millions. Although thieves covet them greatly, they cannot get near them.

During the reign of the Emperor Hsien Fang there lived three powerful robbers who could fly over the roofs and walk up and down the walls of houses. If anyone surprised them they would blow poisonous smoke into his face to make him faint.

These robbers broke into the imperial temple one night and from the altar stole golden incense burners, jade bowls and silver dishes. They concealed them under their shirts and thus climbed up the wall again.

Suddenly they saw an old man with a white beard sitting on the roof-tree of the temple. He pointed his hand at them and instantly the three were pinned down astride the wall and could not get down. Their legs seemed to be nailed to the wall.

When dawn broke, the guardian of the temple found them there. He had them brought down and questioned.

They confessed everything. The guardian of the temple thereupon made a report to the court and by reply was instructed to grant a place of sacrifice to the fox.

Since then he has worked great miracles. By degrees he received the highest official button and the yellow riding jacket.

Throughout Manchuria temples and votive pictures have been set up to him. He is represented as a dignified high Manchu official. The people praying for the granting of happiness or the averting of sorrow are so numerous there that they rub shoulders and jostle each other. In the temple forecourt stands a great incense burner. In it stand veritable forests of incense sticks. The smoke of sacrifice rises from them in thick clouds and the ash of the burnt paper money flutters about like butterflies. Those who pray hold their breath as they fling themselves down and dare not look about. The people refer to the fox as the third father, not daring to utter the word 'fox'. More recently his veneration has spread to eastern Shantung and is now very extensive there.

THE silver foxes resemble the foxes, except that they are yellow or white. They too can intervene in human affairs. There is one kind which can acquire human speech in the space of a year. These are known as the talking foxes. Southwest of Kiauchou Bay there is a mountain on the seashore. It is shaped like a tower and is therefore called Tower Mountain. On top of it stands an old temple with a divine picture which is known as the Old Mother of the Tower Mountain. Whenever a child falls ill in one of the neighbouring villages the magicians order paper pictures of them to be burnt or clay models of them to be erected. As a result the altar and the area around it are covered with hundreds of clay children. Moreover, offerings of paper flowers, clothes and shoes are made to the Old Mother and these likewise are scattered about in colourful confusion. On the third day of the third month and on the ninth day of the ninth month pilgrimages take place. On these occasions plays are performed and the sacred scriptures are read. Moreover, a fair is held regularly. The women and girls from all over the neighbourhood burn incense and submit their petitions. The childless ones pray for sons. They will choose one of the clay children, tie a red thread round its neck, and perhaps even secretly break off a small piece of its body, mix it with water and drink it. Then they pray silently that this child may come to them.

Behind the temple there is a vast cave and this used to be occupied by talking foxes in former times. They would often come out from the cave and sit on the top of a steep rock by the roadside. Whenever a wanderer came past they would say something like: 'Why not stop for a moment, neighbour, and smoke a pipe?' The wanderer would look around in astonishment to discover where the voice came from and would usually be much afraid. Indeed, unless they were particularly courageous the sweat would appear on their skin and they would run away. And the fox would laugh at them.

Once a peasant was ploughing on the mountainside. When he glanced up he saw a man in a straw hat and a grass coat approaching with a hoe on his shoulder.

'Neighbour Wang,' he said, 'smoke a pipe with me and have a little rest! I'll give you a hand with your ploughing then.'

Then he called out: 'Whoa!', the way the peasants do when talking to their beasts.

The peasant looked at the man more closely and discovered that he was a talking fox. He waited for a suitable moment and then struck him a hard blow with his oxhide whip. It hit him squarely. The fox screamed, leapt into the air and made off. He left his straw hat, his grass coat and everything else behind. Looking at these things more closely the peasant discovered that the straw hat had been woven from potato leaves. It had been cut in two by the whip. The grass coat was made of oak leaves tied together with thin blades of grass. But the hoe was a kaoliang stem to which a piece of a tile had been tied.

Some time later a woman in a neighbouring village was possessed. The people pinned up a picture of the Taoist pope but the spirit would not leave her. As no exorciser of devils could be found in the neighbourhood and the plague was becoming unbearable, the woman's relations agreed to send a messenger to the temple of the war god and ask his help.

When the fox heard of this he said: 'I am not afraid of your Tao pope nor of your war god. The only person I fear is your neighbour Wang in the eastern village who once hit me with his whip.'

This was just what the people wanted to hear. They sent to the eastern village and there asked for Wang. Wang took his oxhide whip with him and entered the house.

In a deep voice he said: 'Where, where, where? I have been on your track for a long time. Now at last I have got you.'

Then he cracked his whip. The fox snarled and shot out through the window.

For another hundred years the people told stories about the talking fox and Tower Mountain. One day a skilful hunter came through that neighbourhood and saw an animal resembling a fox with a fiery red fur with grey markings on the back; it was lying under a tree. He took aim and shot off one of its hind legs.

Thereupon the animal spoke in a human voice: 'My weakness for sleep led me into this peril, but no one can escape his fate. If you capture me all you get for my skin is five thousand pieces of copper at the most. Why don't you let me go instead? I will reward you generously and all your poverty will be at an end.'

But the hunter did not listen to him but killed the small fox. Then he skinned him, sold the fur, and true enough he received five thousand pieces of copper for it. That was the end of the spirit.

ONCE there was a man who, together with a few inquisitive friends, often held seances to raise spirits. One day a famous doctor from the Middle Ages appeared. But the words he uttered were crude and uneducated, and his poems did not rhyme properly. He always presented himself immediately when summoned.

Once, when they were in the middle of questions and answers, he rapped the signal: 'I wish to leave.' They asked him where he wanted to go. He replied: 'The Tsien family have asked me to dinner.' After that the desk remained silent. That family lived near by. The friends were curious and therefore walked across to the other house to find out about the business. There they were told that because of some sickness in the family, sacrifices had been made.

The next day the ghost came again. They asked him: 'Did you go to supper with those people?'

'Yes,' was the reply.

'Was the food good?'

'Oh yes, indeed.'

Then they taunted him: 'But these people invited gods, not famous men. They wanted the city god or the god of the field. Why should a famous man like you go and dine with them?'

Thus cornered, the ghost replied: 'I am not really the doctor at all; I am Li Pei-nien from Shantung.'

'And who was Li Pei-nien?' they asked.

'I was a cotton merchant at the time of Kang Hsi and

died on my way to this village. My soul dwells in the little temple by the bridge. In addition to me, there are another twelve homeless souls there. Because we were not guilty of any particular misdeeds we can move freely. We get the benefit of all the offerings made in the village here.'

They asked: 'But surely the offerings for the city god and the other gods are addressed to a particular name. How can you nameless souls mix with those gods?'

The reply came: 'The city god and the others do not enter people's houses. The offerings which are made there are left untouched by them. That is where we benefit.'

They next asked: 'But if the heavenly gods discover that you nameless ones have eaten up their offerings—do they not punish you?'

'What do the heavenly gods care about such prayers! These are merely the customs and habits of foolish men. Frequently demons possess the people in order to extort food offerings from them, and still nothing happens to them. Why then should the heavenly ones care if we benefit from a few food offerings which we did not extort but which were placed there voluntarily? After all, I did not extort the tea and wine from you which you have offered me.'

'In that case,' they went on questioning, 'why did you assume the name of that famous doctor?'

'Your domestic spirit was holding your incantation in his hand, looking for a spirit. But he dared not approach any real saints. So he invariably got one of us thirteen. But since I am the only one who can write a little I have been taking the liberty of answering your summonses. But if I had given you my true name of Li Pei-nien, would you have venerated me in the same way? And then I found that a lot of families here had requested that doctor to write inscriptions for them, so I knew that he was a famous man and I decided to come under his name.'

'But if the likes of you are free to move,' they continued to question him, 'why then do you not return to Shang-tung?'

'There are spirits everywhere in the passes, at the fords and on the bridges. And unless one gives them money they do not let one pass.'

'If I burnt a hundred notes of paper money for you to enable you to return home—would you like that?'

'Yes indeed, thank you very much! But if you want to do me a favour—I would need a further one hundred to pay off the bridge spirit where I have been lodging, or else I shall not be able to part on friendly terms.'

So the man burnt paper money so that the spirit could go off on his journey. Since that day he has never summoned any spirits again.

WHEN a person dies his body is first laid out on his bed, face upwards. He is put into new clothes and an ear of millet is placed by his head and a ploughshare on his chest so that the corpse shall not rise again. Nevertheless, one occasionally hears of a corpse rising. According to old people a corpse rises when it is struck by the breath of living people or when a dog or cat sniffs it. It will then straighten up. If the living person in the room is sitting the corpse will also sit, if a person is standing up then the corpse too will rise to its feet. If the person runs away in fear then the corpse will follow it, as if drawn by some secret force. But such corpses cannot speak.

It is said that, until a corpse is placed in his coffin, the people who keep a vigil must not lie down to sleep feet to feet with the corpse. The reason is that, while a human sleeps, the force of brightness in his body circulates right down to the soles of his feet. Should these accidentally touch the feet of the corpse then this force of brightness would flow into the corpse and mingle there with the force of darkness so that the corpse will seem to come to life again.

It also happens that corpses which have already been buried will not decay but will rise from their graves at night and haunt the living. Those are ghosts. If this goes on for a long time these ghosts gradually change into the spirits of drought which can cause prolonged dry spells. Whenever clouds appear in the sky, promising rain, such a spirit of drought will pick up a broom and sweep the clouds together, piling them on his grave. Then the sky is clean once more and the sun comes out again. There is one reliable way of stopping these spirits of the drought. One investigates whether among the graves of persons recently buried there is one which has the moisture of rain upon it whereas all around everything else is dry. That must be the grave. The elders then summon all the men of the village, the grave is opened up again and the coffin unscrewed. If it is then found that the corpse has not decayed but that white or green hair is growing on it, it is vigorously beaten with sticks and burnt on a fire. This produces a hissing noise. That is why there is a widespread custom in the countryside that, while a corpse lies in state, all brooms are carefully hidden away so he shall not steal one and turn into a spirit of drought. If such a spirit pursues its activities for a long time he may change into a werewolf or into an ogre flying across the sky.

In the Sung period there lived a man who was exceptionally strongwilled. After his death he haunted the place as a ghost and finally turned into a golden-haired werewolf. This werewolf looked like a lion, except that it was much bigger and that its whole body was covered with golden hair well over a foot long. It devoured humans and animals without number. The magicians were unable to subdue it, until one day the saint Wen Chu arrived. He forced the werewolf to submit to him so he could ride on it.

Buddhism has three powerful helpers in adversity, and pictures of all three can be seen in many places, showing them all mounted on animals. The first is the saint Pu Hien, who rides a lion, the next is the saint in the white robes who rides an elephant and is revered as Kuan Yin or the goddess of mercy on the island of Putou in the southern sea, and the third, as we have seen, is the saint Wen Chu on a werewolf.

ONCE there lived in Annam a man whose name was Siu and who sailed the seas as a merchant. One day he was driven off course by a great storm and came to a distant coast. Jagged mountains rose on it, covered with luxuriant green vegetation. Then he caught sight of what looked like human habitations on land. He took with him some food and disembarked. No sooner had he got among the mountains than he saw the openings of caves on both sides, one next to the other, like beehives. The merchant stopped and looked into one of these holes. There were two ogres inside, with teeth like spears. Their eyes were like fiery lamps. With their claws they were tearing a stag apart and devouring it raw. The merchant was terrified and wanted to escape. But the ogres had already spotted him. They caught him and drew him into their cave. The two creatures talked together in animal sounds. They tore the clothes off his body and wanted to devour him. Then he hurriedly produced bread and dried meat from his satchel and offered it to them. They shared it, ate it all up and seemed to like it. They searched his satchel, but he gestured with his hand to indicate that he had no more.

Then he said: 'Let me go! Aboard my ship I have pots and pans, vinegar and spices. With these I could cook fine meals for you.'

But the ogres did not understand what he was saying and were still angry. He therefore tried to make them understand by gestures, and eventually they seemed to get his meaning a little. They followed him to his ship, and he brought his cooking utensils back to the cave, gathered firewood, lit a fire and cooked the remains of the stag. When it was done he gave it to them to eat. The two creatures devoured it with great pleasure. They then left the cave but closed the opening with a large boulder. After a little while they returned with another stag they had caught. The merchant skinned it, got fresh water, washed the meat and cooked several cauldrons full of it. Suddenly a whole herd of ogres came in and devoured the meat. They seemed to enjoy it. They all pointed to the cauldron which seemed to them too small. After three or four days one of the ogres returned with a huge cauldron on his back, and from then onwards this was regularly used.

The ogres now all crowded around the merchant, bringing him wolves and antelopes which he had to cook for them and whenever the meat was ready they called out to him to join them.

Thus several weeks passed and gradually they became so familiar with him that they allowed him to move about freely. The merchant after a while learnt to distinguish the noises they uttered and to understand them. Indeed, before very long he learnt to speak the ogre language himself. This quite delighted the ogres. They brought a young female along for the merchant to marry. But he was afraid of her and dared not come close. But the ogre girl took him by force to be her husband and had much pleasure from him. She gave him precious things and fruit to allure him and gradually they came to be fond of each other like husband and wife.

One day all the ogres rose very early and placed necklaces of gleaming pearls round their necks. They ordered the merchant to cook a large quantity of meat. He asked

154

his wife what was happening.

'Today is a great feast,' she said. 'We have invited the great king to eat with us.'

And turning to the other ogres she said: 'The merchant has no pearl necklace.'

Thereupon all the ogres gave her five pearls apiece and she herself added ten so that he had over fifty pearls. She threaded them and hung the chain round his neck. Each of these pearls were worth several hundred plummet-weights of silver.

The merchant then boiled the meat and with the whole herd left the cave to welcome the great king. They entered a vast cave in the middle of which was a large boulder which was smooth and flat like a table. All round were stone seats; the place of honour was covered with a leopard skin, the others all had stag skins on them. Several dozen ogres were sitting in the cave in orderly rows.

Abruptly a great storm arose, raising the dust, and a monster came in who resembled the ogres in shape. The ogres all stood up in great excitement to welcome him. The great king ran into the cave, sat down legs apart and looked around with large keen eyes. Then the whole herd followed him into the cave. They lined up on both sides of him, looked up to him and crossed their arms on their chests to express their respect.

The great king nodded his head, looked at them and asked: 'Is everybody present from the Wo Mei Mountain?'

Yes, they all said.

Then he caught sight of the merchant and asked: 'And where does he come from?'

His wife answered for him and they all praised his cooking skill. A few of the ogres brought in cooked meat and spread it out on the table. The great king ate his fill and,

155

with his mouth still full, praised the food and commanded that this dish was always to be served to him.

He then glanced at the merchant and asked: 'Why is your necklace so short?'

With these words he took ten pearls from his own necklace, and these were large and round like rifle bullets. His wife quickly accepted them for him and hung them round his neck. The merchant crossed his arms and thanked the king in ogre language. Thereupon the great king left again, riding away through the air on the storm.

The merchant had lived with his wife for four years when she bore him triplets—two boys and a girl. They all had human shape and were unlike their mother.

One day the merchant was alone in his home when a female came in from another cave and tried to seduce him. But he resisted her. The ogre woman grew angry and grabbed him by the arm. Just then his wife returned and the two women began to fight fiercely. Eventually the merchant's wife bit one of the other woman's ears off and after that she left. From then onwards the merchant's wife always guarded her husband and never left him for a moment.

Another three years passed and the children were learning to speak. The merchant also taught them human language. They grew up and became so strong that they ran up and down the mountains as though on level ground.

One day the wife had gone out with one of the boys and the girl and stayed away half the day. The north wind was blowing strongly and there arose in the merchant's heart a longing for his old country. He took his son by his hand and led him to the sea shore. There his old ship was still riding at anchor. He boarded it with his son and after a day and a night returned to Annam.

When he got back he found that his first wife had meanwhile married another man. He produced two of his pearls and exchanged them for such a quantity of gold that he was able to keep an elegant house. He gave his son the name of Panther. When he was fourteen he was so strong that he could lift thirty hundredweight. But he was rough and fond of quarrels. The general of Annam, amazed at his bravery, appointed him a colonel and he so distinguished himself in the crushing of a rebellion that he was made an under-general at the age of eighteen.

About that time another merchant was likewise driven by a gale to the island of Wo Mei.

When he stepped on land he caught sight of a young man who asked him curiously: 'Are you not from the Middle Kingdom?'

The merchant related how he had been driven off course and the young man led him to a small cave in a hidden valley. There he produced stag meat and chatted to the man. He told him that his father had also come from Annam and it turned out that the two merchants were old acquaintances.

'We must wait for the north wind to rise again,' said the young man, 'then I will come and see you off. I will also ask you to give my regards to my father and elder brother.'

'Why don't you come along yourself and join your father?' asked the merchant.

'My mother is not from the Middle Kingdom,' replied the young man. 'She is different in speech and appearance, and therefore I cannot leave.'

One day soon afterwards the north wind sprang up powerfully and the young man went and saw the merchant off on his ship and asked him in parting not to forget his message.

157

When the merchant reached Annam he went to the palace of Panther, the under-general, and told him of his experience.

When Panther heard him speak of his brother he sobbed bitterly. He took leave and, accompanied by two soldiers, sailed out on the sea. Suddenly a typhoon sprang up which whipped the waves till they splashed up to the sky. The ship capsized and Panther fell into the sea. But at once he was seized by a creature and dragged to a beach which seemed inhabited. The creature which had grabbed him looked just like an ogre. Panther therefore addressed it in ogre language. Amazed, the ogre asked him who he was and he told him his whole story.

The ogre was delighted. 'Wo Mei is my old home,' he said. 'It is eight thousand miles away from here. This is the land of the venomous dragons.'

The ogre got a ship and made Panther board it. The ogre then pushed the ship in front of him through the water, so that it cleaved the waves like an arrow. After one night a coastline emerged in the north. There was a young man standing on the beach, looking out to sea. Panther recognized him as his brother. Then he turned to thank the ogre who had brought him there but he had disappeared. Panther now asked about his mother and sister and was told that they were both well. He wanted to go with his brother, but his brother asked him to wait and went off alone. After a short while he returned with his mother and sister. When they saw Panther they both cried with emotion. Panther now asked them to accompany him back to Annam.

But his mother said: 'I am afraid that if I went with you the humans would mock me for my appearance.'

'I am a high officer,' replied Panther. 'The people would

not dare offend you.'

So they all went on board together. A favourable wind filled the sails and they moved over the sea as swift as an arrow. On the third day they reached land. But all the people they encountered ran away in horror. Panther took off his coat and divided it among the three so that they could cover themselves.

When they got home and the woman saw her husband again, she chided him for not telling her about returning home. The relations who called to welcome the master's wife did so trembling in fear. Panther now advised his mother to learn the language of the Middle Kingdom, to dress herself in silks and get used to human food. She consented, but both mother and daughter had men's clothes made for them. Panther's brother and sister gradually turned whiter in the face and soon came to look like the people of the Middle Kingdom. The brother was called Leopard and his sister Ogrechild. Both were of extra-ordinary strength.

Panther did not like his brother to remain so uneducated and therefore arranged for him to study. Leopard was exceedingly gifted. He grasped the meaning of books upon first reading but had no inclination to become a scholar. Shooting and riding were what he liked best. So he made a great military career and eventually married the daughter of a highly respected official.

It was a long time, however, before Ogrechild found a husband because the men were all afraid of their mother-in-law. Eventually one of her brother's subordinates lost his first wife, and agreed to marry Ogrechild. She could draw the string of the strongest bows and at a hundred paces could still hit the smallest bird. Her arrows never fell to the ground without having hit something. When-

159

ever her husband went into battle she would accompany him, and the fact that he ended up as a general was largely due to her.

Leopard was a Field Marshal by the time he was thirty. His mother invariably accompanied him on his campaigns. Whenever a dangerous enemy appeared she put on armour and took up a knife to meet that enemy in place of her son. Among the enemies there was none who did not flee in terror. For her courage the emperor awarded her the title of 'Greatest of Women'.

The history books always tell us that there are very few ogres about. But if you reflect a moment you will find that they are not in the least unusual. In fact, every married man has one such little ogre at home.

To the west of the old capital Loyang there was a derelict monastery. In its grounds stood an enormous pagoda, several hundred floors high. At its top there was still enough room for three or four persons.

In the neighbourhood there dwelt a beautiful girl. One day, in the heat of summer, she was sitting in the court-yard to enjoy the breeze when suddenly a violent whirl-wind sprang up and carried her away. When she opened her eyes again she was at the top of the pagoda. By her side stood a young man in scholar's clothes.

He was handsome and courteous and said to her: 'Heaven has destined us for one another.'

He thereupon produced bread and wine and so they celebrated their wedding. After that he would go away during the day and return in the evening. Whenever he left he closed the openings of the pagoda with stones. He had, moreover, removed several treads of the staircase so that she could not leave her abode. When he returned he always brought wine and food and shared these with the girl. He also gave her presents of face-paint and powder, clothes and skirts, and all kinds of baubles. He would say he had bought them in the market. He also hung up a carbuncle stone so that the pagoda was lit up brightly even at night. The girl had everything her heart desired and yet she was not happy.

Over the months the young man had become so used to her that one day as he left, he forgot to block the windows. The girl secretly watched him go and suddenly saw him change into an ogre with madder-red hair and coal-black face. His eyes protruded from their sockets and his mouth was like a dish of blood. Crooked fangs thrust out from his lips and a pair of wings sprouted from his shoulders. Thus he flew down to the ground and instantly changed back into human shape.

The girl was gripped by horror and burst into tears. She looked down from her pagoda and caught sight of a wanderer down below. She called out to him, but the pagoda was so high that her voice did not reach him. She waved her hand, but the wanderer did not look up. She could think of nothing else but to throw down her old clothes, the ones she had worn when she was carried off. They fluttered down to the ground.

The wanderer picked up the clothes. Then he glanced up to the top of the pagoda and there spotted a minute figure which resembled a girl—but he could not distinguish her features. He thought for a long while. Then suddenly he began to understand.

'Surely,' he thought to himself, 'our neighbour's daughter was carried off by a magic whirlwind. Could she be the person up there?'

He took the clothes and showed them to the girl's parents. When they saw them the parents burst into tears.

Now the girl had a brother who was stronger and braver than anyone far and wide. When he heard what had happened he took a heavy axe and walked up to the pagoda. There he hid in the grass and waited for whatever was going to happen. The sun had just set when a young man appeared walking up the mountain. Suddenly he turned into an ogre, spread his wings and was about to take off. The brother flung his axe at him and struck his arm. The monster uttered a wild scream and made off towards the western mountains. When the brother discovered that the pagoda could not be climbed alone he returned home and made arrangements with several neighbours. The following morning they all returned and climbed the pagoda. Most of the steps were still quite well preserved, and the ogre had destroyed only the top flight. With a ladder it was possible to climb to the top. The brother brought his sister down and got her home safely. And the ogre was never seen again.

In Sian there lived an old Buddhist monk who was fond of roaming through lonely country. On one of his wanderings he came to the Kokonor. There he saw a dead tree which was a thousand feet tall and many yards thick. It was hollow inside so that the light from the sky could be seen falling in from the top.

He had gone on for a few miles when he saw a girl in a red skirt, barefoot and with bare breasts, running up towards him. Her hair trailing behind her, she was running as fast as the wind. In a moment she stood before the monk.

'Have mercy on me and save my life!' she called to him.

When the monk asked her what the trouble was she replied: 'There is a man pursuing me. Tell him you have not seen me and I shall be grateful to you as long as I live.'

And with these words she ran towards the tree and crept into it.

The monk continued on his way. Soon he encountered a man on a caparisoned horse. He wore a golden robe. Across his back hung a bow and on his side he wore a sword. The horse galloped like lightning and with each bound it covered two miles. Moving through the air or over the ground made no difference to it.

'Have you seen a girl in a red skirt?' the stranger asked him. And when the monk replied that he had not seen anything he continued: 'Monk, you must not lie! This girl is not a human but a flying ogre. There are thousands of kinds of ogres and all of them bring ruin to humans. I

164

have wiped out countless numbers of them and my task is well-nigh finished. But this one is the worst. Three times last night I was commanded by the god and have hastened here from heaven. Eight thousand of us have ridden out in all directions to catch this monster. Unless you speak the truth, monk, you sin against heaven.'

Then the monk dared not deceive him any longer and pointed to the hollow tree. The messenger from heaven dismounted, stepped into the tree and looked for the girl. Then he remounted and his horse carried him up through the hollow tree towards its top. The monk looked upwards, and there he saw a red glow escaping from the top of the tree. The heavenly messenger followed it. They rose up towards the clouds and disappeared from sight. A little while later blood came raining down from the sky. No doubt the ogre had been hit by an arrow or had been captured.

The monk later related the story to a scholar who wrote it down.

THE savages in the southwest practise a great deal of black magic. Often they will lure people from the Middle Kingdom by promising their daughters to them in marriage. These wretches must then work for them and the marriage does not in the end take place. Thus there was once a son of poor parents who was pledged as the son-in-law of a savage. He had to work for three years; after that the daughter was promised to him in marriage. The wedding was celebrated and a special hut prepared as their wedding chamber. The bride was beautiful beyond all measure and was eighteen or nineteen years old. In accordance with custom she entered the chamber first, with a lantern in her hand. But when the bridegroom lifted the bed curtains and was about to get on to the couch the girl had disappeared and was not to be found anywhere. The door and the windows were firmly bolted as before and he could not think where she had got to. So things went on for a month. She was there in the daytime and gone at night. But during the day she would not speak a single word to him, and the bridegroom grew suspicious.

There was also a younger sister in the house. She was always coming out into the courtyard to play. At a suitable moment the man began to question her about the whole business. At first she did not want to give anything away, but he gradually won her confidence by giving her sweets. Then she confessed to him that the whole thing was a magic trick. However, if he were to sprinkle the blood of chickens or dogs in the four corners of the house

166

and quickly snatch the bride's clothes she could not then escape from him. He did as the young girl counselled and when the young wife entered at nightfall and closed the door and got into bed he stepped up swiftly and caught her sleeve. However much she tried she could not escape him.

Then she said with a smile: 'No doubt my talkative little sister has told you everything. But it never was my wish to refuse to be your wife; it was my parents' command and I dared not oppose them. But as things have fallen out now heaven has clearly meant us for each other.'

So they really became man and wife and came to love one another more each day. The parents knew about it and secretly hated him for it.

One day the wife said to him: 'Tomorrow is my mother's birthday; you too must give her your good wishes. They will certainly offer you wine and food. Now you may drink the wine but you must not touch the food. Remember this!'

The following day the wife and her husband stepped into the hall to offer their good wishes. The parents appeared to be greatly pleased and offered them wine and sweetmeats. The son-in-law drank but did not eat anything. With gentle words and friendly gestures his parents-in-law continually invited him to help himself. The son-in-law did not know how to refuse. In the end he thought that surely they would not cause him any harm and when he saw fresh and tempting shrimps and crabs on the plate before him he ate a little of them. His wife gave him a reproachful glance. He pretended to be drunk and made as if to leave.

But his mother-in-law said: 'This is my birthday. You

167

must try some of my birthday noodles!'

Thereupon she placed a large dish in front of him, with noodles resembling silver threads, and with rich meat spiced with fragrant mushrooms. Throughout the three years he had spent at the house the son-in-law had never eaten such delicious food. Its perfume rose temptingly to his nostrils and he could not stop himself from picking up his chopsticks. His wife signalled to him with her eyes but he pretended not to notice. She cleared her throat meaningly but he pretended not to hear it. Only when she kicked him under the table did he regain control of himself.

He had eaten less than half his plateful and said: 'I have had enough.'

Thereupon he left with his wife.

'This is a bad business,' his wife said. 'You did not listen to me and now you are sure to die.'

But he would not believe it until suddenly he felt a violent pain in his body which soon became so unbearable that he fell to the ground unconscious. Hastily his wife hung him up by his heels from a ceiling beam, his head downwards, and placed a brazier with glowing coals under his body and stood a large vessel with water and some oil of sesame in front of the fire directly under his mouth. As the fire now warmed his body right through there was a rumble inside him like thunder and he opened his mouth and began to vomit violently. And the things he threw up! A mass of squirming poisonous worms, centipedes, toads and tadpoles plunged into the vessel with the water. His wife thereupon untied him again, carried him to his bed and gave him wine with realgar to drink. After that he felt better.

'What you thought were shrimps and crabs,' his wife said to him 'were in fact toads and tadpoles, and the birth-

168

day noodles were poisonous worms and centipedes. Now you must not relax your vigilance! My parents know that you have not died and they are sure to plot further schemes.'

A few days later his father-in-law said to him: 'There is a tall tree growing on the rock-face in front of the cave with a phoenix nest in it. You are still young and good at climbing. Run up there for me and get me the eggs!'

The son-in-law went home and told his wife.

'Take long bamboo poles with you,' she said, 'then tie them together and fasten a sickle-sword to the end. Here are nine loaves and seven times seven chicken eggs. Take these with you in a basket. When you come to the spot you will see a large nest up among the branches. Do not climb the tree but cut the nest down with the sickle-sword! Then throw away the pole and run as fast as you can! If a monster pursues you throw the loaves at it, always three at a time, and in the end drop the eggs on the ground and run home as fast as you can! In this way you may come safely through the dangers.'

The man remembered this carefully and left. And true enough there was a bird's nest as large as a circular pavilion. He tied his sickle-sword to the pole and, using all his strength, cut the nest down. He then dropped the pole on the ground and without turning his head ran back. Suddenly he heard the roar of a thunderstorm overhead. When he glanced up he saw a huge dragon a hundred yards long and some ten feet in circumference. Its eyes glittered like a pair of lamps and from its mouth came flames of fire. Two of its horns were thrusting downwards. Just then the man threw his loaves into the air. The dragon caught them and took a little while to devour them. But no sooner had the man gained a little headway than the dragon again caught up with him. So he threw up some more loaves and when he had run out of them, he emptied his basket and let the eggs roll over the ground. The dragon had not yet eaten its fill and its mouth was gaping with hunger. When it suddenly saw the eggs on the ground it came down from the air, and because the eggs were scattered all around it was a little while before they were all drained empty. Meanwhile the man made good his escape and reached home.

As he entered the room and saw his wife he said to her between sobs: 'It was a narrow escape and I very nearly filled the dragon's belly. If things go on like this I shall die.'

With these words he knelt down and implored his wife to save his life.

'Where is your home?' his wife asked him.

'My home is a good hundred miles from here, in the Middle Kingdom. My old mother is still alive, but what worries me is that we are so poor.'

His wife said: 'I will escape with you and seek out your mother. Do not worry about being poor.'

With these words she took whatever pearls and precious stones there were in the house, put them in a sack and bade her husband to tie it round his loins. She then gave him an umbrella and at dead of night they eloped, climbing the wall with a ladder.

Then she said to him: 'Put the umbrella on your back and run as fast as you can! Do not open it and do not look round! I will follow you secretly.'

So he turned towards the north and ran as hard as he could. He had run for a day and a night, near on a hundred miles, and had already crossed the frontier of the land of the savages when his legs began to ache and he felt hungry. Ahead of him lay a mountain village. He stopped at the entrance to the village to rest a little, took some food from his pocket and ate it. He looked round but could not see his wife.

Then he said to himself: 'Perhaps she deceived me and is not following me at all.'

When he had finished eating he drank from a spring and then wearily dragged himself onwards. Just as the day was at its hottest a violent downpour suddenly started. In his hurry the man forgot his wife's instructions and opened the umbrella to protect himself against the rain. Then his wife fell out of the umbrella on to the ground, completely naked.

She reproached him: 'Once again you did not listen to me. Now look at the trouble we are in.'

She urged him to hurry into the village to buy a white cockerel, seven black cups and half a piece of red muslin.

'And don't be mean with your money!' she called after him.

He went into the village, bought all these things and returned. His wife tore up the cloth, made a skirt out of it and put it on. They had barely walked a few miles when a red cloud was seen approaching from the south, as swift as a bird.

'That is my mother,' said the wife.

A moment later she was there overhead. Then the wife took the black cups and flung them at her. She flung up seven and all seven fell down again. Then they could hear the mother cry and complain up in the cloud, and then she disappeared.

They continued for about four hours. Then they heard a sound behind them like silk being ripped and there was a cloud, as black as ink, sailing up against the wind.

'Alas, that is my father!' said the wife. 'Now it is a matter of life and death. He will not let us go. For love of you I must now break the most sacred commandment.'

With these words she swiftly picked up the white cockerel, tore off its head and flung it up into the air. The black cloud dissolved and her father's body dropped down by the side of the road, its head severed. Then the woman cried bitterly and when she had finished crying they buried the corpse. They then continued on their way to the man's home. There they found his old mother still alive. They now produced their pearls and precious things, bought a good piece of land, built themselves a handsome house and became wealthy and well respected throughout the neighbourhood.

AMONG the savages in the south there are a great many tribes. There are the Hui, the Li, the Yao, the Babesifu and many others. In Kwangsi they have eighty-three settlements. But the most numerous are the Li. Among them there is a custom that when a girl reaches marriageable age a temporary husband is first of all chosen for her and taken into the house. After a few months the man then gets leprosy or some other bad skin trouble and is sent away. Only then is a proper marriage contracted with a respected family of the same tribe. This practice is known as transferring the leprosy. Unless this is done the girl herself falls ill. For that reason it is impossible to find a proper husband for a girl who has not yet thus transferred her leprosy to someone else.

Once there was a young man in Kweilin. He came from a rich family. And because his teachers treated him too strictly and from time to time his father would punish him he could no longer bear it at home and ran away. He lost his way and came to a settlement of savages and there asked for food. There was an old man who took pity on the youth, invited him to his home and generously feasted him with food and wine.

Then he said to him: 'You do not seem to be an ordinary vagabond. I have a daughter who is just looking out for a husband; I would like to give her to you for a wife.'

The young man reflected that there was already a girl betrothed to him back home. But faced with hunger and cold he agreed to everything. The old man then called the whole household together. A bridal chamber was prepared and the young man led in. The bride was in it already. She was exceedingly beautiful and seemed a good girl.

The night was still and everyone had gone to bed. The two sat side by side in embarrassment, not knowing what to say. The girl sat a little way apart, her face in her hands, sighing bitterly and ceaselessly. The young man was tired from his journey and soon fell asleep. At the first crowing of the cock he woke and saw the girl still sitting there as before.

'It is late and the night is cold,' he said. 'Do you not want to lie down?'

The girl blushed with shame and said among tears: 'This is a wicked marriage. You must not pity me.'

Then she explained to him how things were and added: 'When I saw how young and handsome you were I could not bear the idea of causing your death. I would rather die myself.'

She then asked his name and wanted to know details of his native village. When day began to dawn she gave him some money and urged him to leave. And so he returned home. After about two years the girl fell sick with leprosy. Her parents were angry and thrust her out.

The girl thought to herself: 'I want to see the young man once more, and then I will die.'

So she bore her sickness and set out on her journey. During the day she begged for food in villages and hamlets, at night she rested in caves and ravines. She climbed over mountains and waded across rivers. Wearily she dragged herself on week after week. Then she reached Kweilin. She searched out the house of the young man and called his name, demanding to see him. But the guard

174

at the door upbraided her and turned her away. Then she collapsed by the door, sobbing.

When the young man had returned home he had applied himself earnestly to his studies and had by now passed his first examination. His parents had already chosen a lucky day for his marriage which was to take place the following day. Friends and relations had already arrived to attend the festivities. The father was just then giving a banquet for the guests.

As the young man was sitting down at the table he heard some noise and shouting outside the door. He went out to see what the matter was. And there was the girl, her face covered with festering boils about to burst, her eyebrows gone, her nose fallen in, her lips cracked and her voice hoarse. He stared at her in horror but did not recognize her.

The girl said: 'Do you not remember the time you stayed at our house, two years ago? Now the disease has broken out in me and my parents have cast me out. Now that I have seen you once more I shall die happily.'

Then his memory came back and he said to her amidst tears: 'You were as beautiful as a flower and now you have become like this! However, you did me great kindness and I swear that I shall not abandon you.' So he took the girl by her hand and led her upstairs to the hall to meet his parents and relations.

There he knelt down, asked permission to speak and said: 'Had I not met this girl I should have long died in some ditch. Our happiness today is her gift alone.'

Generously his father said: 'Let her be my son's wife too! When we celebrate the wedding tomorrow it shall be a double wedding. The two women shall be sisters to each other, neither being the principal wife and neither the second wife!'

The friends and relations all agreed and poured out wine to wish them happiness and all the talk at table was about this girl's virtue.

But the girl bowed deep and said amidst tears: 'An evil disease clings to me and I shall die today or tomorrow. How could I bear to be this gentleman's companion and celebrate a marriage to him? All I ask is to be granted a room where I can die in peace.'

The father furtively glanced at the girl and saw that her disease really was evil and that she was not fit for wedding festivities. He ordered a room to be prepared for her to live in, off the back courtyard. A maidservant swept the floor, led her in and spread blankets and cushions on the couch.

That room normally served as a wine store. All round the walls and in the corners stood jars of wine. The girl asked the maidservant about them.

She replied: 'This is good old wine, and whenever you are thirsty you are free to help yourself.'

The following day the wedding took place. The sound of the drums rose up to the sky. Flutes and pipes deafened the ear. The girl heard the merry noise and was sad. Then she remembered the wine. She opened one of the jars to ladle some out. Suddenly she saw a poisonous snake, with white markings all down its body, coiled up in the jar. She recoiled in fright. Probably the jar had not been tightly closed and the snake, searching for food, had crawled in and drowned in the wine.

The girl thought to herself: 'I have heard that snake poison kills humans. Rather than waiting to perish by my disease I will drink the poison and die now.'

She ladled some wine out with a cup and drank as

much as she could. Overcome, she fell back on her couch, pulled her blankets over her and fell asleep.

At midnight the sweat burst out from her skin and trickled down in droplets. There was a strange itching in all her limbs. Much as she scratched herself she could hardly bear it. But gradually her sores disappeared, scabs formed, and as they fell off there was fresh healthy skin underneath. Her hair and eyebrows grew again and before a week was passed she had once more turned from a hideous sight into a beauty. Indeed, she was just as beautiful as she had been before her illness.

When they heard the news the whole household came to congratulate her. The son of the house was beside himself with happiness. Another wedding day was chosen and once more he entered the bonds of marriage with the girl. His first wife, too, was very fond of the girl. They loved one another like sisters, and there was neither envy nor strife between them from beginning to end. The foreign wife bore her husband three sons, all of whom rose to high office and distinction so that the mother was decorated by the emperor on account of her sons. Her fame spread throughout the neighbourhood and everyone said: 'That is the reward of virtue.'

THERE was a man in Taiyüan whose name was Wang. One morning when he was walking in the neighbourhood he encountered a young girl walking alone, who carried a bundle under her arm. With her small feet she only made slow progress. Wang walked faster and caught up with her. She was a charming girl of about sixteen.

He liked the look of her and said to her: 'Why are you about at this early hour, walking all on your own?'

The girl replied: 'Strangers cannot relieve each other's sorrow. Why do you trouble to ask me?'

The young man said: 'What is your sorrow? If I can help you I shall gladly do so.'

The girl replied sadly: 'My parents were desperate for money. They sold me as a slave to a rich man. His wife was jealous; she would scold me in the morning and beat me in the evening. I could bear it no longer and am now running away.'

'And where do you want to go?'

'Lost people have no home.'

Then the young man said: 'My house is not far from here. Would you care to come and look at it?'

The girl consented gladly. The young man took her bundle and conducted her home.

The girl saw that there was no one in the room and asked: 'Have you no wife?'

'This is only my study,' was his reply.

'It is a good place,' said the girl. 'If you pity me and

178

want to save my life you must not tell anyone that I am here.'

The young man promised and hid her in the remote room. Days passed without anyone discovering anything. In the end he dropped a few hints to his wife. She suspected that the girl might be a slave from a great house and urged him to get rid of her. But he would not listen to her.

One day, when he was on his way to the market, he met a priest who looked at him curiously. The priest asked him whom he had just encountered.

'No one,' the man replied.

The priest said: 'You are surrounded by a malign aura. Why do you say no one?'

The young man insisted on his denial.

So the priest left him saying: 'How strange that there are people in the world who go to their death and will not listen to advice!'

The priest's words set the young man thinking and he began to suspect the girl. But then he dismissed the idea: 'Surely she is just a pretty girl. Why should she bring me misfortune? I believe the priest just wanted to make a little money out of me by performing the exorcism.'

When he came to his gate he found it bolted from inside and he could not get in. He wondered who could have bolted it. He therefore climbed over the wall. But the door to the room was also locked. He crept up to the window and peeped inside. He caught sight of a hideous devil, with a blue-green face and teeth like a saw. He had spread out a human skin on the bed. He was holding a brush in his hand and was in the process of painting the skin. When he had finished he dropped the brush, picked up the skin like a garment, slipped it on, and he was transformed into the young girl again.

The young man, having watched this transformation, was greatly alarmed and crawled out of the courtyard on all fours.

Hurriedly he went to find the priest. No one knew where he had gone. He followed his tracks in several directions and eventually found him in the fields. He flung himself down before him and entreated him to save him.

The priest said: 'We shall drive her out. In fact, the creature is hard pressed. At this very moment she is trying to find a substitute and I have not got it in my heart to touch her life.'

With these words he gave him a magic whisk and commanded him to hang it up on the door of the room. As they parted the priest told him to come and see him again in the temple of the green lord.

The young man went back home. He dared not enter the study but slept in the inner room. He hung up the magic whisk.

At about midnight there was a rattling sound outside the door. The young man was afraid to go and look, and sent his wife instead. She saw the girl approaching. But when the girl saw the whisk she dared not enter but remained rooted to the spot, grinding her teeth. It was a long time before she went away.

After a little while the girl returned and said angrily: 'The priest is trying to frighten me off, but I won't stand for it. If he doesn't look out I'll devour him first and spit him out afterwards.'

She grabbed the whisk and broke it in two. Then she broke down the door and entered. She made straight for the man's bed and ripped open his body, tore out his heart and vanished.

The wife called the maidservant. Lights were brought, but the man was dead. His blood was welling from his chest in streams. The wife, horrified, was quietly sobbing. The next morning she sent her husband's brother to inform the priest.

The priest was angry. 'I was merciful to her and now the devil has shown such insolence!' With these words he followed the brother to the house. The girl had disappeared. The priest raised his head and looked around in all directions.

'Fortunately she has not got far,' he said. 'Who lives in the southern courtyard?'

The brother replied: 'I live there.'

'That is where she is now,' said the priest.

The brother was astonished, for he knew nothing about it.

The priest asked: 'Has no stranger entered your house?'

'I have just been to the temple to look for you. I don't know but I will go and find out.'

After a while he returned. 'You are right—there is someone there. This morning an old woman came and asked to be employed as a servant for our staff. The people took her on and she is still there.'

'That's her,' said the priest.

He walked across with them, took up a wooden sword, stepped into the middle of the courtyard and called out: 'Devil's brood, give me back my whisk!'

Inside, the servant grew nervous and paled. She came out of the door and tried to escape. Then the priest struck her. The woman fell down. The human skin peeled off her and she was transformed into a devil, rolling on the

181

ground grunting like a pig. The priest cut off its head with his wooden sword. Thereupon the creature changed into thick smoke which swirled up from the ground. The priest produced a gourd flask, opened it and placed it in the midst of the smoke. The smoke began to eddy, and, just as one sucks in air through the mouth, so the smoke instantly disappeared inside the flask. The priest stoppered it and placed it in his pocket. They all then inspected the human skin—eyebrows, eyes hands and feet, everything was there complete and accurate. The priest rolled it up and there was a rustle as when a picture is rolled up. He placed it in his pocket as well and turned to leave.

But the wife stopped him at the door and with a tear-stained face implored him to bring her husband back to life. The priest protested that this was beyond his powers. The woman began to lament even more bitterly, flung herself to the ground and remained huddled at his feet.

The priest thought for a long time and then he said: 'My skill is not sufficient to raise the dead, but I will tell you of a man who may be able to help you. If you find him and ask him he will surely accede to your request.' When she enquired who it was he replied: 'In the market there is a madman who is for ever rolling about in filth. Why don't you try to move him with your entreaties? But if he sneers at you and refuses you, you must not get angry.' The wife's brother-in-law remembered seeing the madman there and so they took leave of the priest.

The wife and her brother-in-law went there together. They soon saw a beggar who was walking down the street, singing like a lunatic. The phlegm was flowing from his nose and he was so covered in filth that one could not approach him. The woman knelt down and moved up to him on her knees. The beggar laughed: 'Darling, do you love me?' The woman told him of her misfortune. The beggar began to laugh: 'Surely there are enough men about for you—why should that one be brought back to life?' The woman continued to tell him her tale of woe. Then he said: 'How odd to ask me to bring him back to life. Am I the prince of hell?' He pretended to be angry and hit out at the woman with his stick. She bit back the pain and suffered it. Gradually the market people collected and surrounded them like a thick wall. The beggar cleared his throat and spat into his palm. He held his hand out to her mouth and said: 'Eat this!' The colour rose to the woman's face and it seemed as if this would be too much for her. But remembering the priest's words she forced herself and swallowed it. She felt something hard slide down her throat, like a round lump which stuck in her chest.

Then the beggar burst into loud laughter: 'Truly, darling, you do love me!' With these words he rose, walked away and took no further notice of her. She followed him. He entered a temple. She still followed him. But when she entered he had disappeared. The people looked for him in front and behind the temple, but there was no trace of him.

She returned home ashamed and unhappy. Filled with grief over her husband's cruel death and with repentance at the humiliation to which she had needlessly submitted she burst into desperate tears, calling for nothing but her death.

The husband's body was now to be cleaned and prepared for burial. The people in the house were standing a little way apart, watching her, not daring to approach her. But the woman embraced the dead body, tidied its entrails and cried. She cried so violently that her voice stuck in her throat and choked her. Suddenly she felt the lump in her chest rising up and jerking from her mouth, and before she could turn her head away it had dropped into the open chest of the dead man. She stared at it in horror, but in his chest now was a human heart which twitched this way and that. The hot breath of life rose up from it like a cloud of smoke. She was utterly amazed and with her two hands closed up the wound in her husband's chest. She had to press with all her might. As soon as she yielded a little the air would rush out through the crack. So she ripped her silken cloth in two and wound it round him. And as she touched the corpse with her hand she could feel it gradually becoming warm. She covered it with a blanket. And when she came to look at it again at midnight there was breath in the man's lungs and by daybreak he had returned to life. He said he had a confused feeling as though he had been in a dream. Moreover, there was a dull pain about his heart. But the wound had closed up and there was only a scab the size of a coin. In due course the man recovered complete health.

ONCE there was a man who belonged to the sect of the White Lotus. He was good at deluding the masses by black magic and many who were anxious to learn magic skills took him as their teacher.

One day the magician was about to leave. He placed a covered dish in his hall and instructed his apprentices to guard it carefully. He also warned them against uncovering it to see what was inside.

He was no sooner gone than the apprentices lifted the lid and found that there was nothing but water in the dish. On the water floated a tiny little ship made of straw, with real sails and masts. They were greatly astonished and jabbed it with their fingers. The little boat capsized. They quickly righted it again and covered up the dish. But at that moment the magician returned and upbraided them angrily: 'Why did you disobey my orders?'

The pupils rose to their feet and denied everything.

But the magician said: 'You cannot deceive me—my own ship capsized on the sea!'

Another evening he lit a huge candle in the room and ordered them to watch it so that the wind should not blow it out. About the second watch, when the magician had still not returned, the pupils felt tired and sleepy; they went to bed and were soon asleep. When they awoke the candle had gone out. They rose hurriedly and lit it again. But almost at once the magician was back and again chided them.

'But we really did not sleep! How could the light have gone out?'

The magician said angrily: 'You let me walk fifteen miles in the dark, and now you lie to me as well!'

At this, the apprentices were very frightened.

He practised black magic of every kind, far more than can be related.

In the course of time it happened that one of the apprentices made love secretly to the magician's favourite slave girl. The magician was well aware of it but he kept his knowledge to himself and said nothing. He then made the apprentice go and feed the pigs. No sooner had the young man entered the pigsty than he was transformed into a pig. The magician called the butcher to have the pig slaughtered and sold its meat. No one knew anything about it.

Later the boy's father turned up to inquire about him because he had not come home for a long time. The magician turned him away and told him that the boy had long left him. The father returned home and made inquiries about his son wherever he could. But he did not discover anything. In the end a schoolmate who had been secretly informed about the whole business told the father the truth. The father thereupon laid a charge against the magician with the magistrate. But the magistrate was afraid the magician would make himself invisible and dared not arrest him but instead reported to his superiors and requested a thousand armoured warriors. These surrounded the magician's house. He was seized together with his wife and son. They were locked up in wooden cages to be taken to the capital.

The road to the capital lay through the mountains. When they were right among the mountains a giant appeared, as tall as a tree, with eyes like saucers, with a mouth like a dish and with teeth a foot long. The warriors stood there shaking with fear and dared not move.

The magician said: 'That is a mountain spirit. My wife knows how to put him to flight.'

They therefore undid the wife's fetters. The woman took up a spear and advanced against the giant. But the giant turned wild and swallowed her lock, stock and barrel. This filled them all with even greater terror.

The magician then said: 'As he has killed my wife, my son must deal with him.'

So they released the son as well. But he was devoured in the same way. Everyone was watching helplessly.

The magician screamed with anger and said: 'First he killed my wife and now he has killed my son. He shall pay for this! But I'm the only one who can deal with him.'

So they released him too from his cage, gave him a sword and sent him into action. The magician and the giant fought for a while but in the end the giant seized the magician, shoved him into his mouth, stretched his neck and swallowed him, and walked off cheerfully.

It was only later that the soldiers discovered the trick that the magician had played on them.

AT the beginning of his reign Duke Ching of Tsi liked to surround himself with heroes. Three of these were particularly brave. The first was called Kung Sun-tieh, the second was called Tien Kai-wang and the third was called Ku Yi-tse. All three were greatly honoured by the Duke. These honours, however, turned their heads; they were noisy at court and did not behave towards the prince as a prince's servants should.

At that time Yän Tse was chancellor in Tsi. The Duke consulted him about what should be done. The chancellor requested that a banquet be given and all officials invited to attend.

On the table, as the greatest delicacy, stood a dish with four magnificent peaches.

In accordance with his chancellor's advice the duke rose and announced: 'Here is some exquisite fruit, but there is not enough for all of you. Only those most worthy shall eat of it. I myself am the ruler of the country and the head of the princes of the empire. I have succeeded in keeping my possessions and power—that is my claim. That is why I am entitled to one of the peaches. Yän Tse is my chancellor; he arranges our relations with foreign countries and sees that our citizens live in peace. He has made our empire strong upon this earth. That is the chancellor's claim and that is why he is entitled to the second peach. There are now only two peaches left but I do not know which of you are most worthy. You shall each rise to your feet and set out your claims. He who has not

188

accomplished great deeds, let him remain silent!'

Kung Sun-tieh slapped his sword with his hand and rose to his feet. He said: 'I am the Duke's field-marshal. In the south I conquered the kingdom of Lu, in the west I defeated the kingdom of Chin, in the north I captured the army of Yen. All the princes of the east come to this court to acknowledge the primacy of Tsi. That is my claim. I do not know if this entitles me to a peach.'

The Duke said: 'Your merit is great! You are entitled to a peach.'

Then Tien Kai-wang arose, smote the table and said: 'I have fought a good hundred battles in the Duke's army, I have killed the enemy's general, I have captured the enemy's flag. I have extended the boundaries of my ruler's land so that it has grown by a thousand miles. How about my claim?'

The Duke said: 'Your claim is good! You are entitled to this peach.'

Then Ku Yi-tse arose; his eyes were staring and he cried with a loud voice: 'Once when the Duke sailed across the Yellow River the wind and the waves sprang up. A river dragon seized one of the horses of the carriage in its teeth and dragged it away with him; the ferry rocked like a sieve and was about to capsize. Then I seized my sword and hurled myself into the water. I fought with the dragon among the foaming waves. My strength enabled me to kill the dragon; my eyes started from their sockets with the effort. Thus I surfaced again—the dragon's head in one hand and the rescued horse in the other. Thus I saved the Duke from drowning. Whenever our country was at war with its neighbours there was no service that I refused. I would lead the vanguard, I would step forward for single combat, I never turned my back on the enemy.

189

Once the Duke's carriage got stuck in the mud and the enemy pressed hard from all sides. I drew the carriage out and put the enemy mercenaries to flight. Since I entered the Duke's services I have repeatedly saved his life. True, my merits are not as great as those of the Duke and the chancellor, but they are greater than those of the two others. Those two each received their peach but there is none for me. This means that great merit is no longer rewarded and the Duke regards me with disfavour. How can I ever show my face at court again?'

With these words he drew his sword and stabbed himself to death.

Kung Sun-tieh rose to his feet, bowed twice and said with a sigh: 'Our claims do not match up to that of Ku Yi-tse, yet we were awarded the peaches. We have been rewarded beyond our merits. That is a disgrace. It is better therefore to die than to go on living.'

He took up his sword and swung it, and his own head rolled in the sand.

Tien Kai-wang looked up and uttered a sound of distaste. He blew out his white breath like a rainbow and his hair stood on end with anger. Then he drew his sword and said: 'We three always served the Duke with valour. We were united like flesh and blood. Those two are now dead, and so it is my duty not to remain alive alone.'

With these words he thrust his sword into his throat and died.

But the Duke sighed for a long time and commanded that a magnificent funeral be arranged for them.

A gallant hero will put his honour above his life. The chancellor knew that and therefore deliberately contrived so to incite them with the two peaches that the three heroes should meet their death.

190

AT the time of the last emperor of the Sui dynasty the real power was in the hands of the emperor's uncle Yang Su. He was a proud man and a spendthrift. In his hall he kept choirs of singing and dancing girls, and maidservants were always at hand to do his bidding. When the great men of the empire came to visit him he would remain comfortably seated on his couch when receiving them.

At that time there lived a brave hero by name of Li Ching. Wearing simple clothes he called on Yang Su to present him a plan for the pacification of the realm.

He made a deep bow which Yang Su did not return and said: 'The empire is about to be submerged in disturbances; heroes are arising all over the place. You are the highest servant of the imperial house; it would be your duty to rally the brave around the throne. You should not turn people against you by your pride.'

When Yang Su heard these words he pulled himself together and rose from his seat and talked cordially to Li Ching.

Li Ching handed him a document and began to discuss all kinds of things with him. By their side stood a maidservant of quite exceptional beauty. In her hand was a red whisk and her eyes were riveted on Li Ching. Li Ching then took his leave and went back to his inn.

At midnight he heard a knock at his door. He looked outside and saw a figure in a hat and a purple robe, with a bundle on a stick over its shoulder.

When he asked who it was he received the reply: 'I

191

am Yang Su's whisk-bearer.'

She entered his room, and took off her outer clothes and her hat. He then saw that she was a beautiful girl of eighteen or nineteen.

She bowed to him and when he returned her greeting she said: 'I've been in Yang Su's household for a long time and have seen many famous people, but none who was your equal. I wish to serve you wherever you go.'

Li Ching replied: 'The Minister is powerful. I fear we may be inviting disaster.'

'He is a corpse with but a little breath in him,' said the whisk girl. 'There is no need to fear him.'

He asked her name and she replied that it was Chiang and that she was the oldest of her sisters.

Looking at her and seeing her brave behaviour and listening to her sensible words, Li Ching realized that she was a heroic girl, and they decided to escape secretly. The girl with the whisk again put on men's clothes, they mounted a couple of horses and rode off. They were making for Taiyüan.

The following day they put up at a hostelry. They had the beds arranged as they wanted them and put up a cooking stove for their meals. The girl with the whisk was standing by her bed, combing her hair. The hair was so long that it reached down to the ground, and shone so that one could see one's reflection in it. Li Ching was outside grooming the horses. Suddenly a man appeared with a red curly beard like a dragon. He had come on a lame mule and now flung his leather satchel on the floor in front of the cooking stove, picked up a cushion and lay down on the bed watching the girl combing her hair. Li Ching caught sight of him and grew angry. But the girl instantly recognized the stranger for what he was. She signalled Li Ching to control himself, quickly finished combing her hair and tied it in a knot.

She then welcomed the stranger and asked his name.

He said his name was Chiang. 'My name is Chiang too,' she replied. 'so we must be related.'

She then bowed to him as her elder brother.

'How many brothers have you?' she then asked him.

'I am the third,' was his reply. 'And you?'

'I am the eldest girl.'

'What a wonderful thing to have found a sister today,' the stranger said cheerfully.

Then the girl called out through the door to her husband: 'Come inside! I want to introduce my third brother to you.'

Li Ching came in and greeted him.

They then sat down together and the stranger asked: 'What meat have you got?'

'Mutton,' was the reply.

'I am very hungry,' said the stranger.

Li Ching went to the market to buy bread and wine. The stranger pulled out his dagger, cut up the meat and they all ate together. When they had finished he fed the remaining meat to his mule.

Then he said: 'My friend, Li, you seem to be a poor knight. How is it then that you are here with my sister?'

Li Ching told him what had happened.

'And where are you making for now?'

'Taiyüan,' came the reply.

The stranger said: 'Will you get another dish of wine for me? I have some spice here for the wine and you shall join me.'

With these words he opened his leather satchel and took out from it a human head and a heart and a liver.

He carved the heart up with his dagger and the liver also and put them in the wine.

Li Ching was horrified.

But the stranger said: 'That was my worst enemy. For ten years I carried my hatred with me. Today I killed him, and I feel no regret.'

Then he continued: 'You seem to me no ordinary fellow. Have you heard of any hero living hereabouts?'

Li Ching replied: 'Yes, I know of one whom heaven seems to have chosen as a ruler.'

'Who is he?' asked the other.

'The son of the Duke Li Yuan of Tang. He is only twenty years old.'

'Could you present me to him?' the stranger asked.

Upon Li Ching's assurance he continued: 'The soothsayers declare that there is a special sign in the air at Taiyüan. Perhaps it comes from that man. You may wait for me tomorrow at the Fenyang Bridge.'

With these words he mounted his mule and rode off as fast as if he were flying through the air.

The girl said: 'He is not a man who should be crossed. I saw that his intentions were not good. That was why I made an ally of him by claiming relationship.'

Thereupon they left together for Taiyüan and at the appointed place they met the Dragonbeard. Li Ching had an old friend by name of Liu Wen-tsing who was a tent-fellow of the Prince of Tang.

He introduced the stranger to Liu Wen-tsing, saying: 'This stranger can tell the future from the lines in a man's face and would like to see the prince.'

Liu Wen-tsing thereupon took him to the prince. The prince wore quite simple domestic clothes but there was something impressive about his manner which distinguished him from all other men. As the stranger caught sight of him he fell silent and his face turned ashen grey. When he had drunk a few cups of wine he took his leave.

'That is the true ruler,' he said to Li Ching. 'I am almost certain, but my friend must see him too.'

Then he named another day and a certain inn where they would meet again. 'If at the door of that inn you see this mule and a very emaciated ass then you will know that I am there with my friend.'

On the appointed day Li Ching went there and true enough outside the door he saw the mule and the ass. He gathered up his clothes and climbed to the upper floor. There Dragonbeard and a Taoist monk were drinking wine. When he saw Li Ching he was delighted and invited him to sit down and drink with them. When they had drunk enough all three of them set out again to see Liu Wen-tsing. He was just then playing chess with the prince. The prince rose courteously and invited them to sit down.

As soon as the Taoist saw his radiant and heroic nature he was overcome and saluted him with a deep bow, saying: 'The game is over!'

As they took their leave Dragonbeard said to Li Ching: 'Carry on to Sian, and when the time is come ask for me at this or that place.'

With these words he left, puffing.

Li Ching and the girl again packed their things, left Taiyüan and continued their westward journey. At that time Yang Su died and great disturbances broke out in the kingdom.

After a few days Li Ching and his wife arrived at the spot appointed by Dragonbeard. They knocked at a small wooden door and a servant came out who conducted them down long corridors. Magnificent buildings arose before them, with crowds of girl slaves standing in front of them. They stepped into a hall in which the most precious dowry had been set out—mirrors, robes and jewellery were all of a magnificence unparalleled on earth. Beautiful slave girls led them to a bath, and when they had changed their clothes their friend was announced. He entered, clad in silks and fox furs, and in his appearance almost suggested a dragon or a tiger. He was delighted to see them and also called in his wife who was of exceptional beauty. A feast was served and the four sat down at table. The table was covered with the choicest dishes of which they did not even know the names. Beakers and plates and all implements were of gold and jasper, adorned with pearls and precious stones. Two choruses of girl musicians in turn played flutes and shawms. They sang and danced and the visitors felt as though they were transported to the palace of the moon fairy. The rainbow garments fluttered and the girl dancers were of a beauty which surpassed anything on earth.

When they had drunk a few rounds their host commanded the servants to bring in beds upon which embroidered silken blankets were spread. When they had feasted their eyes on everything Dragonbeard presented them with a book and a key.

Then he said: 'In this book are listed the treasures and riches which I possess. I give them to both of you as a wedding present. Without possessions no man can undertake great deeds, and it is my duty to give my sister an appropriate dowry. I had originally intended to take over the Middle Kingdom and put matters to rights. But now that a ruler has arisen already, what else is there for me to do here? The Prince Tang in Taiyüan is a real hero.

He will have put matters to rights in a few years. You two must support him and you will assuredly rise to high honours. You, sister, are not only beautiful but have also good sense. No one but you would have recognized Li Ching's true value and no one but Li Ching would have had the good luck of meeting you. You will share this man's honours and your name shall go down in history. This is all predestined. As for the treasures I have given you, you are to use them to help your true lord. This you must be sure to do! In ten years a glow will arise far away in the south-east, and that shall be my signal to you that I have attained my aim. When you see that glow you may pour a wine offering towards the south-east to wish me luck.'

He thereupon ordered the maidservants and the other servants to salute Li Ching and the girl one after another and said to them: 'These are your master and mistress.'

With these words he took his wife by her hand, they mounted the horses which were being held for them, and rode off.

Li Ching and his wife then moved into the house and were immeasurably rich. They became followers of the Prince Tang, who created order in the empire, and they supported him with their money. Thus the great work was achieved and when the empire was at peace again Li Ching was appointed Duke of Wei and the girl who had held Yang Su's whisk became his duchess.

Ten years later news was brought to the Duke that in the far-away empire across the sea a thousand ships had landed with a hundred thousand soldiers in armour. They had captured the land, killed the ruler and set up their leader as king. The empire was now pacified, and the Duke knew that Dragonbeard had accomplished his work. He told his wife. They put on festive garments and made a wine offering to express their good wishes. Then they saw a red glow shine brightly in the south-eastern sky. Undoubtedly this was the signal sent by Dragonbeard in reply. The two were exceedingly happy.

AT the time of the Tang dynasty there were skilled swordsmen of different orders. The first were the sword-saints. These could change their shape at will and their swords struck like lightning. Before people knew what had happened to them their heads were rolling on the ground. However, these were high-minded men who did not readily get involved in worldly business. The second kind were the sword-heroes. They would kill the unjust and help the oppressed. They carried a dagger concealed at the waist, and over their shoulder they had a leather satchel. By means of magic they could transform human heads into water. They could fly over the roofs and walk up and down walls, and came and went without trace. The lowest kind were the murderers, who could be hired by anyone wanting to be avenged upon his enemies: to them death was an everyday occurrence.

Old Dragonbeard no doubt came halfway between the first and second categories. But Molo, of whom the present story tells, was one of the sword-heroes.

At that time there lived a young man called Tsui. His father was a high official and the friend of a prince. One day the father sent his son to visit a sick friend. The son was young and handsome and highly gifted. He went to do his father's bidding, and as he entered the house three beautiful slave girls heaped red peaches upon golden dishes, poured sugar water over them and presented them to him. When he had eaten he took his leave, and his noble host commanded one of the slave girls, called Rose-Red, to accompany him to the gate. As he walked along the young man continually turned his head to look at her. She smiled at him under her lashes and made signs to him with her hand. First she stretched out three fingers, then she turned her hand three times and finally she pointed to a little mirror which she wore on her chest. As they parted she whispered to him: 'Do not forget me!'

When he got home his mind and thoughts were in turmoil. He sat there absent-minded, like a wooden cockerel. Now he had an old servant called Molo, who was an exceptional man.

'What is the matter, master?' he addressed him. 'Why are you so sad? Will you not confide in your old slave?'

So the young man told him what had happened and also mentioned the secret signs which the girl had made to him.

Molo said: 'The fact that she stretched out three fingers means that she lives in the third courtyard. Her turning her hand three times signifies the number of three-times five fingers, that makes fifteen. And by pointing to her little mirror she meant that on the 15th, when the moon will be as round as a mirror at midnight, you are to go to her.' These words roused the young man from his confusion and he could hardly contain himself with joy.

But soon he was sad again and said: 'The prince's palace is cut off as if by the sea. How could one possibly penetrate into it?'

'Nothing easier,' said Molo. 'On the 15th we will take two lengths of dark silk and veil ourselves in it, and I shall thus carry you there. However, there is a fierce dog guarding the courtyard gate of the slave girl, and this

200

dog is as strong as a tiger and as watchful as a god. No one can pass it. It must first be killed.'

When the appointed day came, the servant said: 'Apart from me there is no one on earth who can kill that dog.'

The young man was exceedingly pleased and gave him wine and meat. The old man then took a sledge-hammer and was gone in an instant.

And before the time of a meal had elapsed he was back again and said: 'The dog is dead, there is no obstacle left.'

At midnight the two wrapped themselves in dark silk and the old man carried the young man over the tenfold walls which surrounded the palace. They came to the third gate which was only ajar. They saw the gleam of a small lamp and they heard Rose-Red sighing deeply. The court-yard was deserted and silent. The young man lifted the curtain and entered. Rose-Red regarded him searchingly for a long while, then she leapt up gaily from her couch and caught him by the hand.

'I knew you were clever and would understand my sign language. But what magic powers have you at your disposal to have penetrated here?'

The young man told her everything that Molo had done for him.

'And where is Molo?' she asked.

'Outside the curtain,' was his reply.

She called him in, gave him some wine in a jasper cup and said: 'I come from a good family far from here. I am kept as a slave in this house under duress. I long to get away, for even though I have jasper chopsicks to eat with and wine to drink from golden goblets, and velvet and silk to clothe myself in, and whatever jewels I desire—all these are but fetters and chains to me. Good Molo, you have magic powers, I entreat you, save me from this misery and I will gladly serve your master as a slave and remember your good deeds as long as I live.'

The young man looked at Molo. Molo was ready to do as she desired. He asked permission to remove first of all her dowry in satchels and sacks. Three times he came and left again before he had finished. Then he took his master and Rose-Red upon his back and with them flew over the high walls. None of the watchmen in the prince's castle had noticed anything. At home the young man concealed Rose-Red in the remotest room.

When the prince discovered that one of his slave girls was missing and one of his fierce dogs had been killed he said: 'This must have been done by a mighty sword-hero.' He then gave strict orders not to allow any news of this to get out and to have the matter followed up secretly.

Two years had passed and the young man no longer thought of any danger. Thus, when the flowers bloomed in spring again, Rose-Red rode out of the city to the river in a light carriage. She was spotted by one of the prince's servants. He reported this to his master, and the young man was summoned to see him. Unable to conceal the business, the young man told him the whole truth.

The prince said: 'Rose-Red alone is to blame. I do not hold you responsible at all. But since she is now your wife I will pardon her too. But Molo will have to pay for it.'

He thereupon ordered a hundred armed warriors to surround the young man's house with arrows and swords and to seize Molo at all costs. Molo took his dagger and flew up to the top of the tall wall. He looked around him like a hawk. The arrows came at him as thick as rain, but none struck him, and in a moment he had disappeared; no one knew where he had gone.

More than ten years later one of his master's servants came across him in the south, selling medicine. He still looked exactly the same as before.

NOTES

1. *Flesh and blood divided by a woman's words.* From oral tradition. 'Roc' is in Chinese Pyong. Cf. *Chuang-tzu*, I, i: 'Nothing but yellow and white things'. The short one does not realize that it is gold and silver.

2. *The child of good fortune and the child of ill fortune.* From oral tradition. The dragon is the symbol of the ruler; New Year is the chief Chinese festival, which young and old celebrate for a whole week.

3. *The nine-headed bird.* From oral tradition. The nine-headed bird is a well-known apparition, rather like our bogeyman. The broken hairpin and other broken pieces of small jewellery divided between lovers are a common motif. The fish is the son of a dragon; dragons, here and frequently elsewhere, are sea-gods, like the Indian Nagarajas. Gourd flasks are a common magic talisman in China; they are also used to confine spirits which then have to serve the owner.

4. *The animals' cave.* From oral tradition.

5. *The fox and the tiger.* From oral tradition. A widespread story, though in China animal tales are rare: 5-8 are four examples.

6. *The tiger's bait.* From oral tradition.

7. *The fox and the raven.* From oral tradition. This is probably the fable from Aesop in a Chinese version. The reference to the 'wisdom of Lao-tse' is from the *Tao-te-ching*: 'Who knows his brightness and still dwells in darkness...' 'Master Chung' was the most faithful pupil of Kuan-tse, renowned for his piety. The raven was known in China as the 'pious bird' because it was said that the young birds would bring up again the food they had eaten in order to feed the old birds.

8. *Why the dog and the cat are enemies.* From oral tradition.

9. *Yang Erlh-Lang*. From the Feng-Shên and the Hsi-yu Chi. Yang Erlh-Lang is a huntsman, always depicted with a falcon and hound. The Hound of Heaven, literally 'the hound that bites the gods' is similar to Indra's hound. The god also appears as the tamer of the spirits of 'Plum Mountain' (cf. full version of story in Fong-Shên). The idea that there were originally ten suns in the sky was also current in the reign of Emperor Yu : in this version the marksman was Hu I or I; here the suns are not shot with arrows but crushed with mountains, in a way reminiscent of the stories of titans. The cricket's song is taken in China for the earthworm's voice.

10. *No Chia*. Sources : *Feng-Shên*, *Hsi-yu-Chi*. 'The eldest daughter of the lord of heaven' : the lord of heaven had nine daughters, who dwelt in the nine heavens : in the Fong Chen Yang Yi, Yin is said to be the surname of No Chia's mother.

Li Ching, the pagoda-bearing king of heaven may perhaps be traced back to the god of thunder and lightning, Indra. The pagoda might then be a misinterpretation of the thunder-bolt Vadira. In this case No Chia could be a personification of thunder; compare the Hindu myth in which Indra Vadi-rapani is persecuted by his youngest brother. The 'golden armlet' is the wheel of Chakra and the 'Great One' (Tai I) the condition of all things before the division into masculine and feminine.

The 'triton' is the Chinese Ya Chia or Indian Yakscha; the 'dragon's tendon' means the spinal marrow, since nerves and sinews were not sharply distinguished. 'No Chia's mother sent him out of the way' : another disaster follows this, when he kills the priestess of the stone god on Skull Mountain with a magic arrow fired at random. This episode is omitted here. 'Three spirits and nine souls' : man has three spirits, usually shown above his head, and nine animal souls.

'That day No Chia had been away in spirit'. The image of the god is only the god's residence, which he can occupy or leave at pleasure. At prayer times he must be summoned by bells and incense. If the god is absent the image is only a piece of wood or painting: hence the apparently disrespectful behaviour of the Chinese when they showed their temples to foreigners.

Bu Hsien, the Boddhisativa on a lion, is the Indian Samantabhadra, one of the four great Boddhisativas of the Tantra school; 'Wen Chiu', the Boddhisativa on the golden-haired mountain lion, is the Indian Mandjusri. The ancient Buddha of Glowing Light, Yan Jung Kiu Fu, is the Indian Dipamkara.

'Black magic': in the *Fong Chen Yang Yi* three branches of the school of Hung Kiun are described: Tsai Kau, practising black magic, and supporting Chon Hsin, led by Tung Tien Yien Chou; Chan Yian, from which a follower of Laotse will abstain, while Yuan Chi Tien Sun ('the first origin') is practised by his pupils in their battles.

'Fire-dates': dates or pastilles of the elixir of life.

11. *The queen of heaven.* Tian Hon or Tien Fe Niang Niang, the Queen of Heaven, is a goddess of seafarers honoured by Taoists and once worshipped in almost all coastal towns. Local sagas are found in her legends relating to the province Fu-kien. She was an officially recognized divinity under the Manchu dynasty.

12. *Nü Wa.* Sources: *Li-chi, Feng-Shèn*, etc. Fu Hsi is the 'life-giving breath'. Nü Wa was originally masculine, but the name, as with many early surnames, was written with a feminine character and gradually led to the personification being thought of as feminine.

Gung Gung, the water spirit, is reminiscent of the Babylonian Tiamat, although there is no question of a direct borrowing. A similar story describes how Nü Wa sent the fire-god, Chou Yung, to conquer Gung Gung.

The story of the revenge of the goddess on Chou Hsin appears in the *Feng-Shên*. Chou Hsin was the last emperor of the Yin dynasty, deposed by King Wu of the house of Chou.

The 'Mountain of Imperfection' is in Chinese Bu Chou Chan.

The transformation of the nine-tailed fox into Ta Chi comes from the *Feng-shên*. The habit of foxes of turning themselves into beautiful girls in order to lure men to their doom is a common theme of stories about foxes.

Bei Gan is the god of wealth.

13. *Confucius*. The stories collected here show how Confucius' personality stubbornly resisted all attempts to build myths around him; only his supernatural knowledge could be turned into a legendary subject.

The unicorn of Chinese myth, or ch'i-lin, is not unlike the mythical beasts of Western legend. It is the king of the four spiritual creatures (the others being tortoise, dragon and feng-hwang or phoenix), and is revered for its mild nature and goodness. The rock crystal or water crystal, as son of which Confucius is described, implies his relationship to the dark lord of the north whose element is water (and wisdom). The Great Mountain or Tai Shan is the holy mountain of Shan-tung, the god of which Huang Fe-hu became.

Wu is a state in the south of ancient China on the Yangtse river. Chou was a half-barbarian state to the south of Wu.

The great Yü was the mythical ruler who first controlled the flow of rivers. *Of the Rise and Fall of Empires*, one of the five classic books, was ascribed to Confucius himself, or at least its essential historical content.

Shih-huang Ti: the famous burner of books and reorganiser of China c. 220 B.C.

The Han dynasty followed the Ch'in dynasty from c. 200 B.C. to 9 A.D.

14. *The god of war*. Source: *San-kuo chih*. The god of war, Kuan Yü, is a historical personality from the period of the Three Kingdoms, which allied themselves to the later Han dynasty c. 250 A.D. Liu Bei founded the Little Han dynasty in Szechuan, helped by Kuan Yü and Chang Fe. Tsau Tsau

founded the kingdom of We and the third was the kingdom of Wu. Kuan Yü became in the course of time one of the most popular figures in Chinese saga, both god of war and saviour at the same time. The conversation of the monk with the god Kuan Yü in the clouds derives from the Buddhist teaching of Kharma. Because Kuan Yü has killed men—even though his motives were good—he must himself suffer the effects of his deeds, even as a god.

15. *Haloes*. Source: oral tradition. The master of heaven, Tien Chi on the Lung Hu Chan, is the so-called Taoist Pope.

16. *Lao-Tse*. The story of his birth is related to that told about Buddha. His white hairs at birth are an explanation of the name Lao-tzu, which can mean either 'old master' or 'old child'.

The Taoists like to emphasize Lao-tse's journey to the west before Buddha's birth, Buddha being only a reincarnation of Lao-tse, according to many of them. The guardian of the Han-Yu pass is called Yuan Yin Hsi in *Lieh-tzu* and *Chuang-tzu*.

On his connection with the *Tao-te-ching*, see the introduction to that book where the story is told at greater length.

17. *The priest of Lau Shan*. Source: *Liao-chai*. Lau Shan: mountains in the Kiau-Chou district, famous since ancient times as the residence of the immortals.

18. *The mean peasant*. Source: *Liao-chai*. 'Taoist' in the original is here translated as 'priest'.

19. *A punishment for disbelief*. Source: cf. *Shên-Chien*, where the disciples are called brothers. Wei Bei-Yang, in the Han period, was one of the founders of Taoist alchemy.

20. *Morning Sky*. Source: cf. *Shên-Chien*. Morning Sky's mother is, according to one tradition, the third daughter of the lord of heaven. Morning Sky (Tung Fang So) is an incarnation of the wood-star or star of the Great Year (Jupiter).

The father king of the east is one of the five elders, representative of wood. The red chestnuts, like the fire-dates, are divine fruit and confer immortality. The dark heaven is the north heaven.

Morning Sky could play the flute beautifully. Flute playing was one of the particular magic practices of the Taoists. Emperor Wu of the Han dynasty was one of the princes particularly interested in magic, and reigned from 180-144 B.C. The three-legged crane in the sun is the counterpart of the three-legged rain-toad in the moon.

21. *King Mu of Chou.* Sources: *Lieh-tzu, Mu t'ien-tzu Chuan, Shên Chien*, etc. Mu of Chou ruled from 1001 to 946 B.C. His name is linked with the tales of the marvellous journeys into the distant lands of the west, particularly to the mother queen (Si Wang Mu). Si Wang Mu was originally the name of a tribe, whose characters meant literally 'mother queen of the west', which opened the way for myth-making around this goddess, who is often compared to Juno. The peaches of immortality resemble the apples of the Hesperides.

22. *Old Chiang.* Cf. *Shên Chien.* In Chinese custom, which coincides with that of other oriental peoples, a broker was always regarded as necessary between the two families before a marriage could be arranged. Elderly women used to do this as a profession.

23. *The kindly magician.* Cf. *Tang Tai Tsung Shu, Shên Chien.* Copper pieces: The old Chinese copper coins with a hole in the centre were strung together 500 or 1,000 at a time, a string being worth about 2s. A million would be worth between £100 and £200, though the value of money was higher in ancient China than today.

Persian bazaar: In the T'ang period there was a lively trade with the west, and Persian bazaars were by no means unusual in the capital, Si-An-Fu in Shen-Hsi.

Herb oven: a kettle on a tripod in which the elixir of life was brewed; the fairies, the dragon and the tiger (the latter being constellations) relate to this. The master required unconditional perseverance in order to create the elixir, and Tu

Chih-chun owed it to him for his kindness to him.

The Prince of Hell, Yan Wang or Yan Lo Wang, is the Indian Yama. There are ten princes of hell, of whom the fifth is the most feared and powerful.

Obduracy: Literally, 'his crime is concealment'. This is a characteristic of Yin, the dark, feminine principle, and the effect of this attitude leads to his rebirth as a woman.

Pinpricks: acupuncture as a treatment for illness.

The purple flames coming out of the oven represent love, which Tu Chih-chun has failed to conquer; he has subdued all other feelings, but love in its highest form of motherly love, remains. The goal of Taoist teaching, as in Buddhism, is the complete destruction of all feelings.

24. *How Mu Lien got his mother out of hell.* Source: oral tradition.

25. *The flower spirits* (cf. *Tang Tai Tsung Shu*). Salix: The names of the flower spirits are used as surnames in China; they are akin to those of the flowers themselves but do not exactly correspond. The play on words is imitated in translation by using the Latin names.

The zephyr aunts: the aunts are called 'Fong' in the original, which in a different script means 'wind'.

26. *The spirit of the Wulien mountain*: The tale comes from Tsu-tsong, to the west of Kiauchou Bay. Wei To is the Sanskrit Veda, a fabulous Bodhisattva who led the armies of the four kings of heaven. His image with drawn sword is placed at the entrance of all Buddhist temples. In China he often has a club resembling a thunderbolt instead of the sword, probably due to a confusion between him and Vaisramana.

27. *The spirit of the Horse Mountain*: Source as 47.

28. *The little dog.* Source: *Liao-chai*.

29. *The dragon emerging from hibernation.* The dragon, chief among scaly creatures and insects, is said by the Chinese to hibernate. It becomes very small when it does so; but at the first breath of spring, it rises to the clouds again in a flash.

The dragon as symbol of the atmosphere is the basis of the idea.

30. *The spirits of the Yellow River.* Source: oral tradition. In place of the old river god Ho Be, popular superstition substituted the Tai Wang. When the railway bridge was built over the Yellow River, these spirits seriously delayed work on it.

'The dammer': Human sacrifices were also common whenever a bridge was built. Such episodes, otherwise rare in China, occurred frequently on the Yellow River.

'Spirit tablet': Divine images first appeared in China with the arrival of Buddhism. The old tradition, preserved by Confucians and in ancestor-worship, regarded a small wooden tablet inscribed with the spirit's name as the spirit's dwelling-place. Plays as part of worship were found in ancient Greece as well as China.

Tsining is a local capital on the Imperial Canal near the Yellow River.

31. *Help in need.* 'Chou Pao accepted responsibility': The local official is responsible for his district in the same way as the emperor is responsible for the whole kingdom. Since extraordinary natural events are a punishment from heaven, there must be a human fault as their cause. This train of thought is akin to the belief that disputes among the gods of the air lead to misfortune, as in the present case; for if men are truly virtuous, the spirits are hindered from such disturbances.

'Gongs and drums sounded at the same time': Literally, cymbals and drums sounded the advance, cymbals the retreat; to sound both at once would confuse the enemy army.

32. *The rejected princess.* Source: *Tang Tai Tsung Shu*; 'tending sheep': sheep are frequently used as a symbol for clouds. (Sheep and goats are indicated by the same word in Chinese.) Chientang: the placename gave its name to the god who ruled there.

33. *The fox hole.* Source: folktale. The fox appears fre-

quently in Chinese superstitions as a demon who can possess humans. A host of hysterical symptoms are attributed to the influence of foxes and weasels, especially if these are of a temporary nature. This tale is a typical example of the way such a case is supposed to develop.

34. *Fox fire.* A similar story appears in *Liao-chai*. The fox prepares the elixir of life by letting his breath rise up to the moon and retrieving it. If anyone can steal it from him, they acquire supernatural powers.

35. *The fox and the thunder.* Source: oral tradition. The dragon, as embodiment of thunder and lightning, hates anything unclean. The fox tries to keep him off with the unclean piece of skirt, at the same time preventing him from rising into his own element, the air.

36. *The kind fox and the wicked fox.* Source: oral tradition. The fox was only recently honoured as a god in China, the belief coming from Manchuria, probably due to Manchurian or Japanese native traditions. The fox spirit is particularly partial to chickens and wine (as in 34). This tale illustrates the type of haunting in which foxes indulge and the confusion which their exorcism requires.

37. *Great Father Hu.* The name of the god is Hu Tai San Ya 'the great third father Hu'. He is the third of his brothers. The sign for Hu is written as a surname, but pronounced Hu =fox. It would be disrespectful to call the god a fox, because foxes, despite their magic powers, are despised. The Manchurian influence is evident in this tale. Temples dedicated to this fox-god were very popular in Shantung in the last years of the Manchu dynasty. The Emperor Hien Fong, consort of the Empress Tsi Hi, ruled from 1851 to 1862.

38. *The talking silver foxes.* Source: oral tradition. The word translated here as 'silver fox', *Pi*, is given as panther elsewhere. The nature of this fabulous creature is somewhere between that of a fox and a panther. 'The old mother' is the mother goddess of Tai Chen, but is also worshipped elsewhere,

chiefly as a goddess who grants the birth of sons.

'Picture of the Taoist pope'. Painted talismans of the Taoist pope, the so-called 'master of heaven' are particularly effective against all kinds of magic. Yuan Ti, the god of war, is also invoked as a saviour in all kinds of need.

39. *The necromancer.* Source: *Shen-tzŭ.* The ghosts are summoned by a planchette, a very popular way of communicating with a ghost in China.

40. *Ghost stories.* Source: oral tradition. Werewolf: in Chinese *Hou,* or sometimes mountain lion.

41. *The land of the ogres.* Cf. *Liao-chai.* The ogres here are the original inhabitants of Ceylon, also called Rakshas, who appear as man-eating monsters in many tales.

42. *The girl who was abducted.* Cf. *Tsŭ-Ssŭ.* The ogre here is a Fe Tien Ya Cha or Yaksha.

43. *The flying ogre.* Cf. *Tang Tai Tsung Shu.* The ogre is also a Yaksha.

44. *Black magic.* Source: oral tradition. Realgar is supposed by the Chinese to be an antidote to poison and to have strengthening properties.

45. *The faithful girl.* Source: oral tradition. A double marriage of the kind described was as unusual in China as in Europe. Concubines were not uncommon, but two first wives of equal rank were unknown.

46. *The painted skin.* Cf. *Liao-chai.* 'Lost people have no home': The ghost betrays its true condition by these words, and because the young man does not turn it away, he falls into its power.

'a substitute': If the ghost could lure another man to his doom, it became free to be reborn.

'the temple of the green lord': The green lord is the king father of the east.

47. *The sect of the White Lotus.* The sect of the White Lotus was one of the revolutionary Chinese secret societies

which regarded Tung Tien Yian Chou as its lord. See note to 10.

'That is a mountain spirit': the mountain spirit is an illusion created by the magician to escape from the soldiers.

48. *How three heroes died for the sake of two peaches.* Cf. *T'ung Chou Li Yuo.* Duke Ching of Tsi (East Shantung) was an older contemporary of Confucius. The minister Yän Tse, supposed author of a book of philosophy, is the same man who hindered Confucius' appointment to an official post in Tsi.

49. *Old dragon-beard.* Cf. *Tang Tai Tsung Shu.* Yang Su died in 606 A.D.

Li Ching (571-649 A.D.) is not connected with Li Ching in No. 10.

Li Yuan (565-635 A.D.) founded the T'ang dynasty. His famous son, to whom he owed his power, the 'Prince of T'ang', was called Li Chi Ming. His father abdicated in his favour in 618. This tale is of course not historical.

50. *How Molo stole Rose-Red.* Cf. *Tang Tai Tsung Shu.* The story is similar to many Indian tales, as in the idea of the sign-language which the hero does not understand but which his companion interprets.